D0786856

The Use
of Science *&*
Technology
in Service *to*
Children
in the Courts

WPI Studies

Lance Schachterle
General Editor

Vol. 6

PETER LANG
New York • Washington, D.C./Baltimore • Bern
Frankfurt am Main • Berlin • Brussels • Vienna • Oxford

Michael Edmond Donnelly

The Use
of Science *&* Technology *in* Service *to* Children *in the* Courts

PETER LANG
New York • Washington, D.C./Baltimore • Bern
Frankfurt am Main • Berlin • Brussels • Vienna • Oxford

Library of Congress Cataloging-in-Publication Data

Donnelly, Michael Edmond.
The use of science and technology in service to children in the courts /
Michael Edmond Donnelly.
p. cm. — (WPI studies; v. 6)
Includes bibliographical references.
1. Child witnesses—United States. 2. Children—Legal status,
laws, etc. —United States. 3. Juvenile justice, Administration of—
United States. 4. Evidence, Expert—United States.
5. Forensic sciences—United States. I. Title. II. Series.
KF9673.D66   347.73'66'083—dc22   2004002882
ISBN 0-8204-1385-2
ISSN 0897-926X

Bibliographic information published by **Die Deutsche Bibliothek**.
Die Deutsche Bibliothek lists this publication in the "Deutsche
Nationalbibliografie"; detailed bibliographic data is available
on the Internet at http://dnb.ddb.de/.

The paper in this book meets the guidelines for permanence and durability
of the Committee on Production Guidelines for Book Longevity
of the Council of Library Resources.

© 2006 Peter Lang Publishing, Inc., New York
29 Broadway, New York, NY 10006
www.peterlang.com

Printed in Germany

Dedication

To my wife Mary Frances, and my children, Katherine and Peter for their steady support, their gentle teasing about "when is the book ever going to be done" and above all else for their limitless love.

To District Attorney John J. Conte for his trust and for the opportunity to serve the families and children of Worcester County.

To Michael O'Leary for his friendship and unfailing encouragement.

To Professor Lance Schachterle and the students of Worcester Polytechnic Institute whose Interactive Qualifying Projects defined the role of science and technology in service to others.

To the children of Worcester County whose strength and resilience motivated the writing of every page of this book.

Table of Contents

Chapter I Introduction 1

Chapter II Children's Rights in American Courts 5

Chapter III The Admission of Scientific Evidence 11

Chapter IV Legal and Scientific Collaboration for Children 21

Chapter V The Twinkie Defense 25

Chapter VI The Prediction of Violence 29

Chapter VII Shaken Infant Syndrome 33

Chapter VIII Biological and Chemical Abuse of Children 37

Chapter IX Bite Mark Evidence 45

Chapter X Cameras and Technology in Courts 51

Chapter XI Biochemical Evidence of the Sexual Abuse of Children 57

Chapter XII Conclusions 65

Chapter I
Introduction

This book seeks to bring my twenty-five years of prosecuting cases concerning children's issues, and my twenty five years as a law professor in children's law, to examine the crucial role of scientific and technological evidence in advancing the rights of children in American courts. My teachers in this subject have first and foremost been the children who I have been fortunate to serve, as they were victims and witnesses in the court process. Their courage in the face of crushing violence outside of court and intense pressure within court has always amazed and encouraged me. It is because of them and for them that this book is written.

I wish to bring to the readers attention through this book the work of a handful of gifted scientists who have done extraordinary work at the crossroads of scientific research, children's law and American public policy in ways that have improved the protection and care accorded children in American courts.

Finally I hope to do with this book one simple thing which was the seed of origin all those years ago when this book was conceived, that is to encourage scientists and lawyers to work toward greater collaboration in advancing the legal and public policy needs of children through the creative use of scientific evidence in children's cases.

Dr. John Caffey, a radiologist working in New York City in the 1940's, decades before the emergence of the national scandal of child abuse, quietly studied the x-rays of children in hospital archives. Doctor Caffey examined the body scans of diseased children, finding numerous broken bones on the children's bodies that had been overlooked in previous radiological studies. As a physician/scientist, Caffey approached his work from the perspective of the scientific method. Never jumping to conclusions, never dismissing possible explanations like the existence of certain bone diseases that could explain the higher then expected frequency of the broken bones on these children's bodies. He moved ahead with his work as a scientist should, not rushing to judgement but carefully examining all the information before him before rendering a conclusion. Only after he had excluded all other known explanations for so many broken bones did he reach his conclusion that many of those broken bones were as a result of abuse of these children. Doctor Caffey found more of these old injuries than he ever expected and he saw that a disturbing number of those children had died as a result of beatings inflicted upon them. In the mid 1940's these findings were nothing short of extraordinary to Caffey. He had not expected these findings, he had looked at every other possible explanation for them, and only in the end of his work did he come to the conclusion that abuse of children, as demonstrated by these radiological findings, was much more frequent an event than previously thought. This conclusion laid the foundation for later work by other scientists that would show how great the risk was to children living in American society and it also laid the foundation for the use of x-ray findings to support prosecutions of child abuse when children could not testify for themselves about their victimization. Decades later I was to be the beneficiary of Caffey's work as I prosecuted child abuse cases.

I prosecuted two adults who were accused of viciously beating a little boy. The little boy was only a few months old and could not testify for himself about who had broken his leg. He had suffered along with other injuries a so-called "green stick" fracture in which the large bone of the leg fragments in a spiral pattern because of the application of opposing forces applied to the leg. This is a wrenching injury inflicted by the twisting of a limb at the same time and in opposing directions. While I would never have the little boy's testimony what I did have was his very bright, very angry and very knowledgeable elderly pediatrician who had clearly read Caffey's work and who was eager to testify that this little boy's injuries could not have occurred as his adult caretakers claimed. They told the doctor that the little boy had fallen in his bath tub. Both adults pled guilty before trial and were sentenced for the abuse of the little boy because of the doctor's willingness to testify against them. This is exactly what I mean to explore, the informed collaboration of physician/scientist, my pediatrician witness and I working together in a way that protected this child from his abusers.

The second case that illustrates this collaboration concerned a prosecution of a teenage girl charged with the beating injury of an infant left in her care. The teenage girl reported that the infant had fallen off a couch and onto the floor when she was caring for her and in that way sustained a serious fracture of the skull. In this case I was able to secure the testimony of an expert witness, a radiologist who was able to testify that the injury to the child could not have occurred in the way the teenager claimed rather, the injury could only have occurred if the child had been swung by her feet like one would swing a golf club and then striking a hard unmoving object like a sink. Fortunately this child and the little boy in the first example made complete recoveries, and the teenage defendant like the adults was found responsible and sentenced. Caffey's work was also known to this radiologist and had helped him to form his scientific opinion that led to the resolution of this case.

Finally this book will explore the successes of scientists including Dr. C. H. Kempe who in 1962 in the *Journal of the American Medical Association* published with others an article in which the term "Battered Child Syndrome" became known to the public. As a result of the work of Doctor Kempe and his colleagues in that article, calling for a national system of reporting suspected child abuse cases, every state in the union came in just a few years to enact mandatory child abuse reporting laws that were to revolutionize the investigation and prosecution of abuse matters concerning children in America. As a prosecutor it was my work to receive those reports of suspected child abuse and then to take them forward to court. Kempe's work changed the lives of thousands of children for the better through his writing and subsequent public policy advocacy. What had previously been hidden and kept from investigation was now in the open.

This, by way of introduction is, what this book will look to do, making the collaboration of scientists and lawyers clear to those who will see it. This book will also explore how these efforts of collaboration can continue and expand for the service of all Americans.

Finally this book will explore the shared intellectual underpinnings so often overlooked between the professions of law and science. The closely reasoned and critical analysis of facts, the deductive reasoning common to both fields and finally an often understated commitment by persons in both fields for order, direction, and service to others. The book will conclude with an exploration of an examination of the drive to care and protect, in this case the drive to care and protect children, that unifies both scientists and lawyers in service to children.

Chapter II
Children's Rights in American Courts

In the springtime of 1964, fifteen year old Gerald Francis Gault and his friend Ronald Lewis were taken into custody by the sheriff of Gila County, Arizona for making an offensive phone call. The United States Supreme Court later described that phone call as "...of the irritatingly offensive, adolescent, sex variety," while another source reported that the boys said to Mrs. Cook, a next door neighbor or Gerald, "Hi Cookie, you've got big bombers." Regardless of the character of that call, Gerald was held in custody by the state with no effective notice to his family of his whereabouts (his older brother was sent out to look for Gerald at the Lewis family's trailer home), with no right to defense counsel and without those other rights that adult defendants customarily enjoy under the United States Constitution including the right to counsel, the right to confront witnesses, the right against self incrimination, the right to cross examine one's accuser and the right to appellate review. Having not been afforded those rights and after a brief hearing in the local juvenile court, Gerald was committed to the State Industrial School of the state of Arizona until age twenty one, six years in custody for his offense.

Why should we care about Gerald and his sentence of six years for an obscene phone call? The case record indicates that Gerald had been in court at least once before for making nuisance phone calls or as the judge recalled it "silly calls or funny calls, or something like that." Perhaps we should first ask, does this sentence seem proportional to the offense charged? The United States Supreme Court did not decide Gerald's case on that point. Still that was my first concern when I read the case back in Law School. Six years in state custody for an offensive phone call. Arizona provided a maximum sentence for this offense when committed by an adult of $5.00 to $50.00 or imprisonment for not more than two months. And Gerald was sentenced to thirty-six times the adult sentence, six years or seventy two months, can that be proportional. The answer to that is that the state is perfectly within its right to impose such a lengthy sentence—exceeding that for adults, because it is believed that children's sentences are curative rather than punitive and hence not cruel or unusual punishment. The answer does not lie in this direction because children's rights have never been found to be fully coequal with adult rights. Still the court did not look to another reason in deciding the case and that was in the errors it found in the juvenile court's failure to protect Gerald's due process rights.

The United States Supreme Court was blunt in its assessment of the juvenile court's handling of Gerald's constitutional rights, writing, "Under our Constitution, the condition of being a boy does not justify a kangaroo court."

First as to the notice of charge the Court concluded that young offenders must be given timely and clear notice of the charges they face. Here Gerald was just taken into custody with no contact given to his family of his whereabouts. That is why his brother was out looking for him. The notice requirement becomes very important to our discussion because it allows children to know exactly what the state claims they did wrong and in turn that allows a child and his or her lawyer to seek expert scientific witnesses to contest that state charge. For example, if the state were to claim that Gerald was drunk while operating a motor vehicle, expert scientific witnesses could review the state's evidence made specific by the court notice requirement and contest the scientific evidence of intoxication usually done by challenging a breathalyzer machine's findings. This case makes such expert testimony possible.

Gerald's case assumes its greatest importance for American children and for those who would assist them through scientific testimony in finding a constitutional right to counsel. No single action by the court could more effectively advance children's rights than this right to counsel. Through this right counsel can examine evidence and seek to defend a child client through the use of expert scientific testimony. The decision in this juvenile delinquency case had far ranging importance in extending right to children in non-delinquency matters as well.

Finally the rights to confrontation of accusers, protection from self-incrimination, to cross examine witnesses and appellate review, none of which were provided to Gerald were accorded to Gerald by this decision. The decision reversed Gerald's sentence and released him and transformed the law concerning children's rights in America as never had been done before. The help that an expert could have offered Gerald is limited only by one's imagination. Consider for a moment, if Gerald's voice had been recorded during the offending call, an expert witness in voice recognition could have been called by the prosecution or the defense to assert or challenge a conviction or if Gerald was limited emotionally or mentally and unable to comprehend the wrongfulness of his actions mental health witnesses could testify to his lack of competency (ability to assist his lawyer in his defense or responsibility (ability to grasp the wrongful nature of his alleged delinquent act of making an obscene phone call). The expert one can see could profoundly affect a child's case.

To fully understand how important expert scientific evidence is to children's rights cases one needs to know the history of those rights and of the extreme limits of those rights in past American legal history.

That legal history of children can best be told through three Supreme Court cases, Meyer v. Nebraska decided in 1923, Pierce v Society of Sisters decided in 1925 and Prince v. Massachusetts decided in 1944.

Meyer was a case like Pierce and Prince that was to greatly shape the course of children's rights in America and also like Pierce and Prince it tellingly was not about children's rights at all but rather about the rights of adults who's property interest or religious interest were indirectly involved with children's interest. In point of fact, these three great constitutional law cases that form the foundation for children's constitutional rights in America did not even have any child litigants involved in them.

Consider Meyer, he was an instructor at the Zion Parochial School in Nebraska who taught bible stories to ten year old Raymond Parpart in German. For teaching in German, which was outlawed by Nebraska in the anti-German furor after the World War, he faced criminal charges including fines and a jail sentence of up to thirty days in confinement. The court, in explaining Meyer's right under the due process clause of the Fourteenth Amendment, that right being to earn a living, in his case as a teacher of German also came to write "…it denotes not merely freedom from bodily restraint but also the right of the individual to contract, to engage in any of the common occupations of life, to acquire useful knowledge, to marry, establish a home and bring up children, …". From this language, in this a criminal case, lawyers and court were able to find a protection for the right of parents to educate their children within their own choosing. This was significant because, while it sets children's rights always in the hands of others, here their parents subject to state review, it is the first clear expression of a constitution right on behalf of children. Note the children, whose education the case discusses were not even litigants in the case. The court went on to strike down Meyer's conviction and the Nebraska law holding that due process protects one in, among other things, securing a living. The expression even in this level of removal for a body of children's rights become important because it allows lawyers to expand this language into other areas of litigation and in that way to include scientific evidence to support that expanding body of constitutional protection for children.

In the case of Pierce v. Society of Sisters decided in 1925, we have one of the greatest living images I know concerning religious freedom. A group of Roman Catholic nuns took their case to the United States Supreme Court seeking to keep their parochial school open. The sisters were opposed by the state of Oregon which had passed the so-called Compulsory Education Act, a thinly veiled piece of know-nothing legislation that would force families to send their children to public schools only and so effectively force the closing of all religious and private schools including the sister's schools. That the sisters were vindicated by the court's finding the act to be unconstitutional because it violated the sister's due process rights, their right to operate their school is noteworthy but more important to our consideration is that this the second important case concerning children's rights was not decided on the basis of protecting children's rights and as in the previous case of Meyer children were not even litigants in the case. Children were not accorded basic rights accorded adults.

Pierce v. Society of Sisters is important to us because of language use in the case to vindicate the sister's rights which came to be used by later cases to assert children's legal interests. That language which came to be used again and again by courts across the years and across the country was these "The child is not the mere creature of the states; those who nurture him and direct his destiny have the right, coupled with a high duty, to recognize and prepare him for additional obligations...."

This language, seeing the child as having independent indeed transcendent rights suggesting an autonomy beyond the state and even the interests of his or her family's was, I suggest, nothing short of revolutionary. Before this children were not talked about as having rights that could be divergent from the state's power to supervise or the family's right to direct their upbringing. This language was to be used in so many settings for children including abortion notification cases of minor girl's parents before the allowance of minor's abortion. But the key element here is a concept of children actually having rights, not a concept by any reasoning evident in earlier American law. For those who would seek to litigate children's rights including those who would use expert scientific testimony these words were the authority to go forward on developing a body of law establishing children's rights.

The final case in this early legal triumvirate is Prince v. Massachusetts decided in 1944. In this case Sarah Prince the aunt and custodian of nine year old Betty Simmons appealed her conviction for violation of Massachusetts child labor law. The aunt had taken nine year old Betty out on the streets of Brockton, Massachusetts to sell the "Watchtower" and "Consolation" magazines. Aunt and child were Jehovah's witnesses and disputed the conviction claiming, that selling the papers on the street did not violate the child labor law but rather that this act was a permissible exercise of the aunt and child's religious freedom under the First Amendment to the United States Constitution. The court upheld the aunt's conviction and brushed aside the claim of free exercise of religion on the child's behalf. Again while this case went on to become crucial in the development of children's rights the child was not a litigant in this matter as in the two previous cases. In language that has been used again and again by courts in cases concerning education, medical care, and numerous other areas of concern for children the court wrote "Parents may be free to become martyrs themselves. But it does not follow they are free in identical circumstances, to make martyrs of their children before they have reached the age of full and legal discretion when they can make that choice for themselves…." This language again underlines the rights of children separate from their parent's choices in certain select situations. This language by no means terminates parental authority and control of children but it does mean that such control and not be unlimited. For cases in which children would seek a legal redress this language has been used to give children authority to protect their rights with or without parental assent. For expert witnesses who might be called on children's behalf this and previous cases of Meyer and Pierce complete this developing body of law establishing children's rights in an albeit indirect (no child litigants involved) way.

The turning point for this matter of children's development of their own rights in context of family in the state comes I believe in the case of Wisconsin v. Yoder decided by the United States Supreme Court in 1972. In Yoder the court was met with a question from members of the Old Order Amish Religion who objected to the state of Wisconsin's requirement that all children including Amish children attend private or public schools until they reached age sixteen. The Amish challenged the law arguing that such compulsory school will put effectively destroy their faith community because it would require Amish children to attend public high schools rather than to end their public school at the end of the middle school and then to come into the Amish community as full members living and working in the Amish farming community

An expert witness was called to support the Amish claim that the added time in high school would destroy their community by taking their children away from formative training in these years within the community itself. Doctor John Hostetler an expert on the Amish society testified that to force the Amish children to go through the compulsory high school attendance would "result in great psychological harm to Amish children, because of the conflicts it would produce; but would, in his opinion, ultimately result in the destruction of the Old Order Amish church community as it exists in the United States today." Doctor Hostetler was joined by another expert Dr. Donald A. Erickson "an expert witness on education, also showed that the Amish succeed in preparing their high school age children to be productive members of the Amish community." These experts one in education and the other in religious history play crucial roles in the trial of the case and they were noted by the court in its decision ruling for the parents in their dispute with the state of Wisconsin. These experts show what impact testimony can have in advancing the rights of children. Their testimony carried the day in excusing the Amish children from compulsory high school education. In a noteworthy dissent by Mr. Justice Douglas he wrote "...I think the children should be entitled to be heard. While the parents, absent dissent, normally speak for the entire family, the education of the child is a matter on which the child will often have decided views. He may want to be a pianist or an astronaut or an oceanographer. To do so he will have to break from the Amish tradition." With these words Justice Douglas gave encouragement to litigators who would seek to vindicate children's rights, be those rights shared by parent and child or just child alone. The point here is that the United States Constitution is not just for adults but for children as well. Dr. Hostetler and Dr. Erickson in the humanities have in this case much to teach us about testimony from any number of sources including the sciences and they show us that expert testimony when prepared and presented effectively can give voice to children who might not otherwise be heard.

Chapter III
The Admission of Scientific Evidence

To truly understand the way that scientific evidence is admitted in American courts one has to understand the extraordinary story of James Alphonso Frye, adulterer, convicted murderer and beneficiary of scientific evidence testimony from one Doctor William Moulton concerning his novel procedure, the "Scientific Blood Pressure Deception Test." For James Alphonso Frye a "Test" that might have saved his life.

James Alphonso Frye's story begins in Washington, DC on November 25, 1920 with the murder of a prominent physician in that city, Dr. Robert W. Brown. Early on, James was a suspect in the murder. He was arrested for the murder of Doctor Brown and he gave a confession for that murder to Paul W. Jones of the Metropolitan Police for the District of Columbia on August 22, 1921. James was indicted by a grand jury in the District of Columbia for the murder of Doctor Brown. His case went to trial in the middle of a Washington DC summer for four days, July 17 through July 20, 1922, with the jury returning a verdict against him for murder in the second degree after less than one hour of deliberation. Those four days of James's trial and the creative defense raised by his lawyer, though not enough to prevent his conviction, shaped the process for admission of scientific evidence in America for the next seventy years. The so-called Frye case, taking James's last name gave birth to the standard for scientific evidence, the so-named Frye Rule. The specifics of that murder case from a summer trial so long ago are crucial to our future admission of scientific evidence even though the Frye Rule has been superseded by subsequent case law. Consider the defense and James's case.

James challenged the prosecution's case against him with a range of creative defenses. James's first line of defense was an alibi defense; "I wasn't there, I was somewhere else, I could not have committed the crime." This must've been a sensitive defense to raise because his highly skilled court-appointed defense counsel Richard W. Mattingly summoned a woman friend of James, Mrs. Essie Watson asserting that he spent the night of Doctor Brown's murder alone and in the exclusive company of Mrs. Watson. At the time of the murder James was married. This clearly raised the side issue of James's adulterous relationship with Mrs. Watson. As trial lawyers will be quick to tell you, one might have a theory of their case and they may have identified a witness they expect will advance that theory of their case, but actually getting that witness into court and on the witness stand, under oath and testifying is not as easy as it sounds. Mrs. Watson, perhaps understandably, failed to show up for court on that July day. Mattingly had subpoenaed Mrs. Watson, along with other witnesses for his client's defense and her failure to show up must have been a harsh blow to the defense. The court records indicate that Mattingly forcefully argued for a continuance urging the court to grant a continuance because of Mrs. Watson's "reported illness" that prevented her from attending the trial on its scheduled day. Mattingly's request for a continuance was denied. This moment for a litigator who has spent so long in constructing a case can be nothing short of gut wrenching. From the actions that followed those moments were exactly that, gut wrenching for Mattingly and his client, but they did not falter. Mattingly argued that James's confession had been improperly obtained by the police and that it should therefore be excluded from the trial. Remember that this case was tried a good 30 to 40 years before the major criminal procedures cases such as Miranda was decided by the United States Supreme Court. Mattingly failed on his plan to challenge Frye's confession and the confession was ruled to be admissible evidence in the case.

At this point in the case Mattingly and his client were in serious trouble. The alibi defense had failed because a key witness for the defense had failed to appear and the defendant's confession was coming into evidence in the prosecutor's case. Still to his credit Mattingly did not falter. Mattingly then attempted his most creative move yet, the effort that would make the case so groundbreaking in the area of scientific evidence. He offered to the judge expert testimony in Frye's defense from Doctor William Moulton. Even from the time span of over eighty years this bold move still strikes me as creative and audacious—the work of a skilled lawyer who just would not give up on his client's behalf. We can see from the record that Mattingly had summoned Doctor Moulton into court and from this we are safe in concluding that Frye and his lawyer had planned this defense in depth and well ahead of the date of trial. Perhaps they could not overcome the "illness" and hence unavailability of Mrs. Watson. Remember that if she were to admit to having spent the night with a married Mr. Frye she could expose herself to public embarrassment by the prosecution over her conduct as some states, even today, have laws for the prosecution of adultery. Not being undone by this loss Mattingly had developed a defense in depth, raising the expert testimony of Doctor Moulton that he hoped would exonerate Frye. Mattingly planned to call Doctor Moulton to the stand and have him testify that he had developed what he claimed was a new scientific test for truthfulness that he called "the systolic blood pressure deception test," an early version of what came to be known as a lie detector. The scientific claim from Doctor Moulton was that if a person were to lie his body would react in a measurable way, here a change upward in that person's blood pressure. Doctor Moulton claimed that while perhaps new and untested, his test had the ring of truth because it was based on sound scientific principles. But Mattingly was even more inventive than one would have expected. A trial attorney would make an offer of proof to the trial judge stating why the new evidence should come into evidence. Here Mattingly was going for the big moment, the grand gesture, the final knockout of the prosecution's case. Mattingly proposed to have Doctor Moulton hook Frye up to his systolic blood pressure deception test machine in front of the very jury itself and to have Doctor Moulton render his finding before the jury's very own eyes. This was nothing short of great theater, great showmanship and great nerve on counsel's part to offer such a courtroom performance. Perhaps poor Mattingly went just a step too far with the in court demonstration, we will never know, but we do know that the trial judge threw Mattingly's offer of Doctor Moulton's test out of court

The exclusion of Doctor Moulton testimony was followed by the conviction and sentencing of James Alfonso Frye for the second degree murder of Doctor Brown. It was at this point, on appeal that the rule of the Frye case came into being. In challenging his conviction Frye addressed the court's rejection of Doctor Brown's expert testimony. Arguing that the trial judge erred in denying Frey this evidence. The hope of Frey was to reverse his conviction based on the courts rejection of this scientific evidence.

Unfortunately for the defendant he was also too loose on his appeal as he had on his trial. In rejecting Frye's appeal the court wrote of scientific evidence "...the thing from which the deduction is made must be sufficiently established to have gained general acceptance in the particular field in which it belongs." With these words the Frye rule was established. The two parts of the rule were first "sufficiently established" a term that later practitioners were to note has very little specificity for future cases and "... in the particular field in which it belongs," with to determine what "the field" meant. For the next is seventy years courts would struggle with these two parts of the test as they tried to apply the law of Frye to all kinds of evidence. It needs to be noted here that lawyers and judges were being called to answer these legal questions with no uniform knowledge of science. This was just not contemplated in the court's decision, but judges did their best to apply the rule. From the trial of Frye through the next seventy years of legal practice lawyers attempted to use scientific evidence in creative ways to advance the interests of their clients. The personal pressures of each litigant, in particular Frye, matched with the skill of his lawyer and a scientific expert produced a dramatic example of how lawyers and scientists can cooperate to advance the law and justice. This is a model that can be used to meet the legal needs of children.

In the case of Daubert V. Merrell Dow decided in 1993 we can see just how expert witness evidence can assist children in court and we also see the new standard for the admission of scientific evidence after the Frye standard was supplanted.

Consider the facts in the Daubert case and how they're so uniquely relevant to children's cases, while still being applicable to all scientific evidence issues in American courts. In Daubert, the plaintiffs parents in this civil case sought to prove that their children had suffered severe and life impairing birth defects as a result of their mother's consumption of medication during pregnancy, manufactured by the defendant Merrell Dow, that was injurious to the unborn.

Jason Daubert and Eric Schuller, the child litigants who brought this lawsuit through their parents, were both born with serious birth defects. The lawsuit claimed that the defendant, Merrell Dow Pharmaceuticals Inc., had manufactured an anti-nausea medicine known as the Bendectin. Bendectin was a prescription drug sold as an anti-nausea treatment by Merrill Dow. During a lengthy discovery period the parties exchanged information about their claims and counterclaims prior to going to trial. In the course of that discovery time Merrill Dow requested summary judgment, arguing that the cases should be dismissed because of the failure of the plaintiffs to state a proper claim. Merrell Dow offered its own expert, a physician and epidemiologist, Doctor Stephen H. Lamm, who through a sworn affidavit stated that he had reviewed all of the medical literature concerning Bendectin and human birth defects from over thirty published studies concerning over 130,000 patients. He claimed that the reports indicated to him that no findings had appeared indicating Bendectin to be a human teratogen (a material capable of causing malformations of fetuses). Based on his review of these findings Doctor Lamm offered his expert opinion that Bendectin use during the first trimester of a woman's pregnancy had not been shown to be at risk for causing human birth defects.

In a creative use of expert testimony, the children and their parents did not contest the conclusions of Doctor Lamm. The children and their parents instead countered by arguing through eight of their own scientific experts that Bendectin could cause birth defects, based on "in vitro" (test tube) and "in vivo" (live) animal studies which suggested a link between Bendectin and fetal malformations. These plaintiff's experts also claimed that pharmacological studies of the chemical structure of Bendectin showed similarities to the structures of other drugs known to cause birth defects. Finally these plaintiff's experts conducted their own "re-analysis" of previously published epidemiological studies which they concluded supported their claim that Bendectin was harmful to fetuses.

The Federal District Court, after consideration of both sides' arguments, granted Merrell Dow summary judgment over the children and parents. The Federal court stated that scientific evidence is admissible only if the principle upon which it is based is sufficiently established to have general acceptance in the field to which it belongs. "See the Frye case. Remember at this point that this conclusion of the Federal District Court comes from the Frye case. The Federal District Court concluded that the proper "field" for inquiry as to the scientific evidence concerning Bendectin was epidemiological (human statistics) studies of the drug to prove causation of the birth defects. Therefore, the children and parents claimed evidence based on animal–cell studies, live–animal studies, and chemical–structure analysis could not, according to the Federal District Court, be raised as an issue upon which a jury could decide the case. What the court was saying here is that the evidence was not sufficient to give this case to a jury to decide because the requirement of Frye "general acceptance" in the relevant "a field" had not been established by the children and parents plaintiffs. Finally the court rejected the claims of the children and parents experts of epidemiological analysis based on recalculation of previous studies because those recalculations had not been published and subjected to peer review.

The children and parents appealed the Federal District Court's decision without success to the United States Court of Appeals for the Ninth Circuit. That Appeals Court in affirming the District Court's decision to grant summary judgment for Merrell Dow again relied on the Frye case. The Appeals Court added that methodology diverged "significantly from the procedures accepted by recognized authorized authorities in the field... and not be shown to be 'generally accepted as a reliable technique'." The children and parents' arguments had come to an end. The case would as others had before it have ended here but for the fact that the United States

Supreme Court had expressed an interest in the matters raised and accepted the case for review.

The Supreme Court noted that the *Daubert* case raised issues that had been sharply disputed and in need of resolution concerning the application of the "general acceptance "standard in the *Frye* case.

The United States Supreme Court in *Daubert* wrote about the significance of what the litigants ask them to consider:

> In the 70 years since its formation in the *Frye* case, the "general acceptance" test has been the dominant standard for determining the admissibility of scientific evidence at trial.

The court was well aware that it was being asked to move away from the seventy-year legal tradition based on *Frye*. The crux of the plaintiff's argument turned not on the longevity of the rule or even its relative utility, but rather whether the rule had been superseded by the adoption of the new Federal Rules of Evidence. The court concluded that the newly adopted Federal Rules did in fact supersede the rule in *Frye*, ending that seventy-year rule and radically changing the practice of scientific evidence admission in American courts. Quoting from Rule 402 of the Federal Rules the court noted:

> All relevant evidence is admissible except as otherwise provided by the Constitution of the United States, by Act of Congress by these rules, or by other rules prescribed by the Supreme Court pursuant to statutory authority. Evidence which is not relevant is not admissible.

The court then went on to define that key term of "relevant evidence" as that which has "any tendency to make the existence of any fact that is of consequence to the determination of the action more probable or less probable than it would be without the evidence. The court went on to conclude that the basic standard of relevance was a liberal one to be followed in this case

The court went on to consider a second rule from the Federal Rules, Rule 702 concerning expert testimony. The rule provides:

> if scientific, technical, or other specialized knowledge will assist the trier of fact in issue, a witness qualified as an expert by knowledge, skill, experience, training or education, may testify thereto in the form of an opinion or otherwise.

As the court pointed out, Frye and the "general acceptance" standard was completely left out of this new rule. The court went on to fashion the second part of the law concerning the admission of scientific evidence in Daubert that is in addition to relevancy a "reliability" test is required. The court in Daubert wrote:

that the Frye test was displaced by the Rules of Evidence does not mean, however, that the rules themselves place no limits on the admissibility of purportedly scientific evidence. Nor is the trial judge disabled from screening such evidence. To the contrary, under the rules, the trial judge must ensure that any and all scientific testimony or evidence admitted is not only relative but reliable.

To relevance the court through the Rules added the requirement of reliability. But this second requirement of reliability is a significant challenge. What the court has done is to require the trial judge in cases concerning scientific evidence assess that evidence on its own scientific reliability before accepting it or rejecting it as legally admissible evidence. Consider that again, the measure of reliability has to be determined by the scientific basis underlying the proposed evidence. This may turn out to be a harder thing to do than deciding if certain evidence is accepted in a particular field of knowledge (Frye). The court has developed a more demanding test of the court's powers than Frye ever did and with that comes the possibility of extreme variations from judge to judge it admission of the same evidence. The court though was greatly optimistic about the application of this rule, writing: "We are confident that Federal judges possess the capacity to understand this review."

Note that some kind of review of proposed evidence is needed here just as it was Frye. Courts have to screen offered evidence of all kinds to make sure that the fact finding is fair and that error does not enter into the court's finding. Just as there was in the Frye test, the Daubert test will not be without disputes. Scientists don't agree on these matters and of necessity the court in Daubert has now placed judges in the position of determining scientific reliability. Consider the directions that Daubert gives the jurists:

> ordinarily a key question to be answered in determining whether a theory or technique is scientific knowledge that will assist the trier of fact will be whether it can be (and has been) tested.

But how valid is the testing required to be? Does the testing need to be done by peers or by the evidence in question's proponent? Were the methods of testing valid? These are difficult questions that scientists spend their whole professional lives wrestling with and now the courts' judges are called to make decisions on these matters. Peer review is therefore a helpful gauge of scientific reliability, but not an infallible one. Today's court of law would not seek to reject Einstein's theories of space and time but in the early development what court would accept? Yet, if courts relied on early "peer review" of these bodies of knowledge, that is practically what the court would do, rejecting later accepted science when pier review was not done.

Does all this difficulty in reaching a conclusion on reliability mean that the test is unworkable? I think the clear answer to that is of course no. This test has and will be applied, but, and this is a very important "but," this new test will ultimately call for greater scientific literacy on the parts of lawyers and judges in using this new evidentiary standard. The rules of evidence themselves urge a liberal interpretation of these evidence testing mechanisms, and if anything, this is going to mean greater rather than lesser admissions of scientific evidence in American courts. A court in Daubert addressed just this concern of greater scientific use when it wrote:

> Respondents express apprehension that abandonment of "general acceptance" as the exclusive requirement for admission will result in a "free–for–to all" in which befuddled juries are confounded by absurd and irrational pseudoscientific assertions. In this regard respondent seems to us to be overly pessimistic about the capabilities of the jury and of the adversary system generally. Vigorous cross examination, presentation of contrary evidence, and careful instruction on the burden of proof are the traditional an appropriate means of attacking shaky but admissible evidence.

The court points out the direction of this type of evidence and that the limitations imposed by Frye are going to be relaxed. The judge's procedure here is a two-step test. First, is relevancy and second is reliability. No more do courts have to select a particular field of science and see if that particular field has pressed "general acceptance" on the offered scientific evidence. This new Daubert test will make the admission of scientific evidence. easier for practitioners than before because it simplifies the analysis and lowers the hurdle for admission. In the long run this is a process that could make for greater admission of scientific evidence in children's cases as well as others in American courts. This is a change in the law and if it is responded to wisely, it can improve the system of justice for American children through a wise collaboration of scientists and lawyers who will use the new law in service to children.

Daubert allowed greater latitude for the children and their families to make their claims. For Jason Daubert and Eric Schuller this was an important decision and it was also an important decision for other children in America.

For those who would seek to offer expert testimony in the spirit of Frye and Daubert it should be known that after seventy years of relative stability under the Frye rule courts are reassessing the procedures for scientific evidence. The Federal Rule therefore needs to be considered in the planned introduction of expert evidence. For purposes of this discussion we will close our review of this, a clearly evolving area of law. For experts who would go to court for their "first time in court" this is the point to start from, does the witness have expertise on the problem at hand. The answer for that "first time" expert depends on knowledge and experience evaluated by legal council and offered on litigants behalf. Preparation, preparation, preparation of witnesses is the key to success.

Chapter IV
Legal and Scientific Collaboration for Children

The best way to understand what is meant by the phrase "legal and scientific collaboration" is to step away from the law itself and to look at the history of science itself.

There is no better starting point in this examination than Thomas S. Kuhn's The Structure of Scientific Revolutions, written in 1962 and revised in 1970. Kuhn was a historian of science and the Laurance S. Rockefeller Professor of Philosophy at the Massachusetts Institute of Technology. Kuhn's work is important in understanding the link between the law and science because it revealed the developmental nature of science, always changing, and more process than form, given over to break-throughs in understanding that periodically change the scientific landscape. This view of science as always changing and in flux is starkly at odds with the general sense some have of science as fixed and immutable. The deeper understanding of this turbulent revolution driven area of human endeavor, science, has broad impact on courts that look to science to give them certainty in expert opinions, It's not that these expert opinions cannot be given, rather it is that scientific knowledge is always developing in explaining more of human experience. The effect of this on courts is that they become arbiters of what is and is not for lack of a better term "good science," i.e., what will and will not be admitted into evidence. To do this efficiently and to encourage lawyers and scientist to work together productively, especially on new and novel scientific evidence an informed understanding of this changing nature of science is crucial. To avoid mistakes in the future admission of scientific evidence courts must, as the court in the Daubert case said, use care. "Respondent expresses apprehension that abandonment of 'general acceptance' as the evidence requirement for admission will result in a 'free for all' in which to be befuddled juries are confounded by absurd and irrational pseudoscientific assertions." This leads one to ask what exactly did Kuhn say that could avoid this morass that Daubert cautioned against.

Kuhn wrote that the vast majority of what we understand to be science is what he called "normal science." By this Kuhn wrote "normal science means research firmly based upon one or more past scientific achievements, achievements that some particular scientific community acknowledges for a time as supplying the foundation for its further practice." From this definition one can see that Kuhn addressed the crucial issues in both Frye and later Daubert, those issues being "particular scientific community"…and "supplying the foundation for its further practice" (in this context read "reliability"). Both Frye and Daubert called on judges to admit or reject evidence after a finding that a "scientific community" has some level of acceptance for an idea offered to the court as scientific opinion and that such evidence has some measure of reliability. Remember in this regard the words of Daubert "…apprehension that abandonment of 'general acceptance'… will result in a 'free for all' in which befuddled juries are confounded by absurd an irrational pseudoscientific assertions." Kuhn remember was not writing for courts or lawyers but rather for those who would understand the history, indeed the revolutionary nature, of science. He is pointing out that much of science is in the normal area, and that while courts want and expect certainty, they often face changing theories Beyond these issues which one could say can be reasonably explored by skillful cross examination by opposing counsel, what if science someday reaches a new and revolutionary conclusion about for example, at what temperature water boils. What if tomorrow a new breakthrough indicates that water can boil at a much lower temperature. Rather than saying the boiling point of water is at issue what if the asserted scientific evidence was "the earth moves around the sun not the sun around the earth." Could a court grasp such an incomprehensible realignment of our thinking, such an "absurd and irrational pseudoscientific assertion." The issue of what is acceptable science and admissible scientific evidence is much more subtle and more subject to change than the law expects. This is Kuhn importance, how are we to understand these revolutions in science, Consider in Astronomy, the claim that the earth moves around the sun. Would that have been conceivable in the 10th century? Galileo wrote, "Facts which at first seemed improbable will, even on scant explanation, drop the cloak which has hidden them and stand forth in naked and simple beauty."

A court would have rejected Galileo's assertion in its time as "absurd" and not accepted by "the scientific community," hence could this happen again with other "new" scientific findings? The answer would be yes. If this is so how do we overcome this inherent risk in new and yet to be accepted scientific conclusions? To this, I suggest, Kuhn provides the answer.

Kuhn wrote about the accepted rules in science as "these are the community's paradigms, revealed in its textbook, lectures, and laboratory exercises. By studying and by practicing with them, the members of the corresponding community learn their trade." Notice how similar Kuhn's words are to Frye and Daubert in looking to the proper scientific "community" to learn what is accepted in that" community "or field and therefore what might be accepted into evidence. The revolutionary thing Kuhn wrote is what happens when the "community's paradigms" are challenged and rejected. Consider Galileo in this regard. Kuhn wrote "Normal science does not aim at novelties of fact or theory and, when successful, find none. New and unsuspected phenomena are, however, repeatedly uncovered by scientific research, and radical new theories have again and again been invented by scientists." Of this revolution Kuhn wrote "Furthermore, the change in which these discoveries were implicated for all destructive as well as constructive...that gain was achieved only by discarding some previously standard belief or procedures and, simultaneously, by replacing those components of the previous paradigm with others." The revolution that these paradigm changes cause two distinct problems for courts who would seek to use scientific evidence. First the "precision" and by that I mean the accuracy for describing an item or event may be accepted but that "precision" of description is subject to refinement even to rejection as scientific knowledge develops. In short there is a built in possibility of imprecision even error in what was claimed to be unshakable in science. Secondly these major shifts in knowledge are met with skepticism by scientists until they become accepted by the community. This means that courts may see the confusion and reject new and valid scientific findings. It is new materials not yet understood by a large enough community or not seen as reliable by the court that is at risk. Kuhn has identified a major problem in the acceptance of scientific evidence by nonscientists, but his work suggests a solution.

Kuhn wrote of science that "In a science, on the other hand, a paradigm is rarely an object for replication. Instead, like an accepted judicial decision in the common law, it is an object for further articulation and specification under new or more stringent conditions." This is the key to Kuhn's importance in the development of law and science for children's law. He did see the links between the two fields of human knowledge and he by this insight suggested how that fields could work together. Kuhn's mention of the common law and its development in parallel form with science gives us a model for working together from one legal or scientific precedent and the next just as occurs in the law and it went to Kuhn called "normal science." That Kuhn's comments also suggest an understanding of the parallel developments of revolutionary ideas paradigm shifts in science and law. In the law there are cases that rearrange the legal process like Gault did for children's law that are like new scientific paradigms that restructure scientific knowledge. To see this is to see at heart that scientists and lawyers are doing one fundamental thing, speaking the same language. That language is the application of earlier findings to current problems to achieve a proper outcome. Each person in this collaboration is in the same effort to order human knowledge and in doing so to understand human experience and practice. These professionals are really working in one same intellectual effort. Therefore if the court is called to examine a proposed piece of scientific evidence under the current standard of Daubert and the Federal rules the scientists, the lawyers and the judge have a framework to build on. That framework and the mutual language of human knowledge drawing on past precedents to shape future decisions is the key to the collaboration that we seek to encourage. The recognition of the link between science and law, building human knowledge in solving human needs, is crucial. Kuhn has the last word here in addressing legal and scientific issues in collaboration when he wrote "Paradigms gain their status because they are more successful than their competitors in solving a few problems that the group of practitioners has come to recognize as acute." This should be the model for collaboration, a shared understanding of mutual traditions and goals, framework and language. Understanding that science and law will change gives court the intellectual flexibility to be open to new and yet to be accepted scientific evidence while still excluding the flawed and error ridden claims.

Chapter V
The Twinkie Defense

A Twinkie has been defined as a "Golden sponge cake with creamy filling." Invented on April 6, 1930 by the Hostess Company and baked by Continental Baking Company this so called "junk food" is in an oblong shape, with a size of 4" x 1" and comes in packages of two and it is reported to have an exceptionally long shelf-life. The Twinkie gave its name to a highly criticized criminal defense from the 1979 prosecution of one Dan White, a San Francisco city supervisor who was charged with the murder of San Francisco's mayor George Moscone and supervisor Harvey Milk. The so-called Twinkie Defense is, I would suggest, emblematic of the risks inherent in the use of scientific evidence, risks I suggest that can be averted with planning and public education. These risks were best expressed in the language of the Daubert case when the court wrote "Respondent expresses apprehension that abandonment of "general acceptance" as the exclusive requirement for admission will result in a "free for all" in which befuddled juries are confounded by absurd and irrational pseudo-scientific assertions." These matters of risk as the court wrote, of "pseudo-scientific assertions" can be avoided by, I suggest informing people about what really did happen in the handling of this case.

First it should be noted that the murders of George Moscone and Harvey Milk occurred on November 27, 1978 in San Francisco's City Hall. White's actions in the murders showed a high degree of planning. He planned and did in fact take along with his gun an extra supply of bullets. To avoid detection White climbed through a window in city hall and in so doing he avoided metal detectors at the doors of city hall. Finally White shot the men nine times. The importance of these observations concerning White's planning is that California at the time hade a rule for "Diminished Capacity due to mental illness" defenses in criminal cases. In fact what California law allowed and what White's defense achieved was that White not only avoided a mental illness commitment but also he was convicted of the lesser offense of manslaughter and avoided the greater offense, conviction of two murders. It is how this defense developed and how it was used that made Twinkie Defense become so important to our considerations and to the history of science in courts.

White's lawyer started in on the development of his defense and during his defense meetings with his client it was apparently observedthat White was a great consumer of junk food, sugar-heavy foods including Twinkies. The defense having made these observations and knowing that "Diminished Capacity" was possible chose to offer scientific evidence, social science evidence, from a mental health professional Doctor Martin Blinder. It is critical to note that the defense did not claim that the Twinkies and other junk food, as many in the public later came to believe, resulted in a mental impairment of White but rather that his high level consumption of such food could be seen as an indication of a long standing depression that White suffered. White's defense lead the jury to conclude that he was incapable of the premeditation required for a conviction of murder. It is at this point that the public confusion about this case develops. The outcome of a manslaughter finding suggested to many that the jury had found the defendant guilty of the lesser charge because of perceived prejudices on its part against gay individuals. It was understood that Harvey Milk one of the victims was gay. Further scorn for the verdict came to be directed toward what was perceived as a trivialization of the court process by what was understood to be the "Twinkie Defense" rather than a mental illness defense of depression leading to "Diminished Capacity." These perceptions colored the public's understanding of the case and raised doubts about the integrity of scientific evidence in courts for years to come.

The perception of the public becomes a crucial matter here because in this case the term the "Twinkie Defense" comes to symbolize to many what is wrong with the law and scientific evidence. Protests and demonstrations follow the White verdict. Because the public was so outraged with this verdict and, because as some observers have suggested a.) the perception that the jury had minimized the seriousness' of the crime because one of the victims was gay and b.) because of a perception that this was a junk science, California voters in 1982 overwhelmingly voted to approve a proposition that eliminated the "Diminished Capacity" defense.

My concentration here is on the perception that the so-called "Twinkie Defense" was preposterous and that it revealed to many proof of their worst fears that lawyers and their scientific collaborators would twist the truth to secure their own narrow goals. Note first that the defense never did propose a "Twinkie Defense" rather they advanced a legitimate mental health defense as was allowed in California law at the time of diminished capacity based on the defendant's perceived depression expressed by his extreme eating habits. Secondly, the "Twinkie" or the defendant's observed consumption of the

Twinkie was only made as one element of a diagnostic presentation that suggested the defendant's claimed depression. How the question must be asked, could such a stretched conclusion have occurred and the answer to that lies in a very disturbing perception of science in the American public. This disturbing perception has serious consequences for the future of our proposed legal and scientific collaboration.

Consider the work of John D. Miller of Northwestern University on American's shocking ignorance regarding knowledge of science in daily life. Miller has researched for a number of years the public knowledge of key issues in science that occur in a public policy context. He has, for example, explored public knowledge regarding nuclear energy when that was critical. Such an issue occurred when he asked Americans if they knew what Strontium 90 was when issues concerning nuclear fallout was in the news or DNA when stem cell issues were in the public domain through the press. Millar's finding were shocking, they included a.) that only about 10% of Americans knew what radiation was, b.) that fewer than one third of Americans could identify DNA as a key to heredity and c.) that one adult American in five thought that the sun revolves around the earth, an idea that the scientific world rejected before the start of the 17th century (see Galileo). Couple this with recent surveys that suggest that disturbingly high numbers of Americans believe that major drug companies and the American Medical Association are hiding cures for cancer to advance their own financial interests and one begins to see how ignorance i.e., the sun revolves around the earth and unfounded suspicions, i.e., drug companies suppression cancer cures suggest that the public is not disposed to understanding or accepting science in court cases.

This becomes a clear problem because how then can a lawyer and scientist realistically expect to speak to a jury of every day Americans and expect to be understood if not actively suspected of lying. I suggest the antidote to this lies in exactly this kind of legal and scientific collaboration in educating Americans.

This problem with the public's perception of science and law raises precisely in the kind of issue that the legal and scientific collaboration that we have discussed can respond to and ultimately correct...

Courtrooms and the media coverage of the trials in those courtrooms have become the public square for much of American life. Whether one considers the media event for the O.J. Simpson trial or less known civil or criminal matters the interest of the public is intense in following these matters. In a trial the issues are presented to a finder of the facts, either a judge or a jury and the communication of these proceedings extends the hearing to the wider reaches of the nation. This combination of public interest bordering on entertainment allows for the chance to educate those who will listen. Consider the specter of a high profile child abuse case like the Michael Jackson trial. The key is not the verdict, guilty or not guilty, rather the key is people who would not otherwise hear expert testimony about child abuse matters. The use of experts in these cases can inform and educate juries and the public on crucial issues. This public role of the trial as part of a wide public forum for education should not be underestimated. These trials become larger than the litigants as they catch the public eye and lay before the public sensitive issues concerning children. Consider what a vehicle for public enlightenment these trials can become. Would it be possible to educate those Americans who still think the sun moves around the earth or those Americans who don't understand the role that DNA plays in heredity and stem cell research? This kind of broad exposure is precisely what is needed to inform public debate on crucial issues including but not limited to those of American children.

This education begins right at the point that a lawyer and a scientist begin to speak one to the other about their concerns. That is the very start of the educational process, from one professional to another. That this process can be horribly misconstrued as it was in the erroneously named Twinkie case is a reason for concern, but it is not a reason to stop working to use scientific knowledge to serve litigants, including child litigants. For each person that concludes the court process is bankrupt for allowing a "Twinkie Defense" there are other members of the public, in this case the jury, who sat and listened to the evidence and reached a verdict that was permitted in law and based on scientific evidence. The verdict, any verdict may or not be popular, but that is not the point, rather the point is that the law gave a jury a chance to listen to and then decide a case on properly admitted evidence. That is all any litigant child or adult can ask and that with all its imperfections is still an extraordinary thing. Court can secure justice and also be a vehicle for public education.

Chapter VI
The Prediction of Violence

No area in the fields of law and science has greater importance to children that the prediction of violence. Whether in a court's consideration of returning a young child to a parent's custody, where that parent may present a risk to the child's well being and life or whether in a court's decision to place a youthful offender in the custody of a state youth agency or a state adult correctional agency, the role of expert mental health witnesses is of breathtaking importance. Privately lawyers and judges will say to one another that these cases are the ones that most often leave them sleepless at night. Quietly judges will say that these cases test their training and souls in ways that they never imagined before taking the bench as jurists. How then can science, social science, address these very personal and professional concerns for those called to make decisions about children's lives in such intense ways?

Doctor John Monahan of the University of Virginia's School of Law has been writing and teaching for over two decades in this area and I believe he provides invaluable assistance to those who must, in American courts make these decisions. Monahan's work has influenced a generation of social scientists and clinicians in responding to the pleas of courts for guidance in these cases. In ways that are at once ethically sensitive to the needs of the litigants while at the same time assisting courts in reaching informed decisions, Monahan's work focuses on observed data such as past history of violent behavior or its absence. Monahan's work encourages these scientific expert witnesses to present their observation to courts while at the same time leaving the decision in the hands of the only one, a judge, who is allowed by law to make those decisions. Monahan's work assists court in making those decisions—but it does not make that decision for the judge. I have actually seen judges become unnerved by this process, saying things like "tell me what you think I should do" or "what is your opinion...is the person dangerous or not." But these questions miss the point on expert witness, any expert witness cannot make the ultimate decision in these mattes because the law does not allow them to do this, such an action would usurp the role of the judge as the final arbiter of this decision. The law does not allow an expert to overstep his or her bounds in this regard. The question then remains: if an expert does not answer these crucial matters with an opinion how can that testimony help a court? The answer to that that the expert can give a judge evidence that is better than opinion, he or she can give the judge facts upon which to base his opinion, the best grounding of any judicial opinion possible that will anchor a courts decision against the "wind and rain" of an appeal.

To weather these storms of appeal Monahan's work offers the most elegant of response to the question, will a person be violent in the future? His response as I have read it and as I have seen it given by witnesses in court is to look to past observations to understand the promise of future behavior. Characterized as an "actuarial response" to the question of future violence these experts offer what any other scientists does the observations of prior experience, in this case among other things the individuals past violent action if any, and a presentation of that past experience of the individual before the court in the context of known actuarial data about human behavior. At first hearing this response I know that I was taken back as was the judge I was before as we consider the risk of future violence presented by a young person charged with murder. To me, and I sensed to the judge, seeing future risks of violence was a mental health issue and not an actuarial one. To us an actuarial analysis signals life insurance and premium calculations but not violent behavior. In this lies the elegance of Monahan's work and its importance to children in this area. The observation of past behavior is the best; one might suggest the only guide to future behavior. Monahan has given us what human knowledge is best at, observing the past to understand the future.

Monahan's work suggested a number of areas that he felt were relevant to the prediction of violence. Those areas were (1) past criminal history (2) age of the accused (3) sex (4) race (5) socio-economic status and employment stability and (6) opiate or alcohol abuse. Using an actuarial model Monahan claimed that these factors had a correlation to future violence. It is interesting to note that mental illness was not seen as one of the factors and that all of the factors were subject to direct observations or relatively easy verification based on an individual's self reporting.

For our purposes of legal and scientific collaboration for children Monahan advances a scientific construct, "actuarial analysis" of past behavior leading to violence prediction that gives courts a firm basis upon which to render informed decisions. In cases that I have handled when mental health experts have offered evidence based on a knowledge of Monahan's work, judges frequently express an initial anxiety about not being given a specific opinion about whether or not an individual will or will not be violent in the future. After time I have seen judges come to understand that if they listen carefully the actuarial data, in particular a past history of criminal violence is crucial to help them to make their decision. Remember here that the prediction of future violence is a particularly controversial area of the law indeed many well informed lawyers and social scientists reject the whole premise that one can or that one should consider future violence in a court proceeding. Not withstanding these very reasonable and informed objections I believe the Monahan's work at the least advanced the field by directing the focus of the courtroom presentation on generally verifiable data.

For children Monahan's work suggests that scientific evidence can be presented in a responsible way; without a clinician offering an opinion on future violence but leaving that up to the court to decide. As I said before I have seen this kind of evidence and I have been impressed with its value. In the area of a youthful offender's potential for future violence the testimony sticks mostly to the past history of violence. Defense and prosecution are free to argue their own conclusions from that history in an attempt to shape the court's decision but the evidence is generally not in dispute.

In conclusion Doctor Monahan's work is an example of legal and scientific collaboration that seeks to answer serious concerns of courts on verifiable data. The novelty if one will of using an actuarial analysis rather than a mental illness approach is I suggest refreshing and offers greater transparency for those involved in these matters. Monahan is, I would argue, in that line of scientists who have offered the court guidance based on their understanding of the scientific method in their field of knowledge that serves court and children for the better.

Chapter VII
Shaken Infant Syndrome

Dr. John Caffey, a radiologist working in New York City in the 1940s, presents us with perhaps the most compelling story of the dogged pursuit of scientific evidence in service to children in American courts. Caffey's work, which we will discuss, formed the basis for later radiological practices that revealed the harm that can occur to very young children in shaken infant syndrome. Consider how Caffey did his work and how it led to such breakthroughs for children.

In 1946 Doctor Caffey published a study entitled "Multiple Fractures in the long Bones of Infants Suffering from Chronic Subdural Hematoma." Caffey's work was based on years of examining archival radiological studies of infants in which partial and full body x-rays had been taken of these children. Again and again Caffey found evidence in the x-rays of earlier and often numerous broken bones in the bodies of these children. Like a good medical detective, Caffey noted that these findings had often been left uncommented on and in a number of cases the children involved had died of unexplained causes. True to the best in the scientific method Caffey did jump to a conclusion that these children had suffered unspeakable violence at the hands of their parents, though he later came to hold that opinion, the evidence was there in the x-rays. Caffey instead of moving in a rash fashion read the x-rays, the medical histories when available and the medical literature regarding unexplained broken bones. His first stop was to consider disease conditions that could explain these multiple traumatic breaks on the bodies of those little children. Among other diseases, he looked at brittle bone disease, an affliction that results in an extreme weakness in human bones that gives over to massive bone breaks under the slightest of most innocent forces, like bumping into a chair of dropping a heavy item accidentally onto a foot. Still not willing to rush to a conclusion, that the breaks had been inflicted by parent/caretakers, Caffey pulled back from advancing the opinion that abuse had been involved in the injury of many of these children. This reservation was perhaps finally overcome as it should in all forensic findings not by emotion but by reason and factual findings that could not be explained by any other source than by violence exerted against the bodies of young children up to and in some case to the death of young children. These matters had apparently lain untouched not investigated and not prosecuted. The power of Caffey's work was that he handled these most painful of findings as a scientist, leading to integrity in his work that lasted.

From a practicing point of view I saw the burning power of Caffey's work in the person of an elderly pediatrician. I was preparing her to testify in a horrific child abuse case I was prosecuting on the very eve of the birth of our first child, our daughter Katherine. As I talked to the elderly pediatrician I asked how she could be so certain that the break in the leg of my child victim had been inflicted. I was prosecuting the little boy's mother and father for the abuse of the little boy. The doctor absolutely exploded at me saying how I could be so dull. She went on to mention the extreme nature of the broken bone, a green stick fracture that was based, as she noted, on the laws of physics and could only result from opposing forces. She continued that the medical history the mother and father gave of the little boy's supposed slip and fall from a bathtub could not explain the x-ray findings of opposing force and a torquing pressure that had shattered, like a splintering of a green stick, a green stick fracture that had damaged the little boy's leg. Finally my witness referenced the medical literature in the field that supported her conclusions and she mentioned to me a rather young and rather overwhelmed young prosecutor the work of Doctor John Caffey.

The doctor's information was for me highly persuasive. After I talked to her on that Friday afternoon in preparation for a Monday morning trial I went home to my wife who was expecting, at any moment, the birth of our first child. As my wife and I rushed to the hospital in the early morning hours of Sunday morning we were overwhelmed with joy for the birth of our daughter Katherine. It was not until a few hours later when Katherine and my wife were both well and settled in the hospital that I had to face the prospect of a jury trial on that little boy's case. I have always believed that the pediatrician/witnesses words, including her mention of Doctor Caffey, saved the day for the child and the trial. I was able to tell the two defense attorneys what my witness had emphatically told me and that she was prepared to testify to in our prosecution.

Both defense lawyers wisely moved to avoid the trial and entered guilty pleas on both defendants followed by sentencing. This was a powerful lesson in the power of expert scientific evidence and in the strength of a committed witness supported by sound scientific findings.

Such finding lead Caffey to write in 1972 "During the last twenty-five years substantial evidence, both manifest and circumstantial, has gradually accumulated which suggests that the whiplash-shaking and jerking of abused infants are common causes of the skeletal as well as cerebra-vascular lesions, the latter...the most common cause of early death." Caffey's work had developed over those twenty-five years. His writing now gave force and direction to other radiologists in this area of childcare while it retained its fact based scientific method of critical questioning of supposed abuse. Because of this critical approach Caffey's writing were particularly influential in revealing to doctor, lawyers and ultimately court what had always been there before then, a history of physical abuse of children much greater than many had ever expected.

Growing out of this strong critical foundation based on the scientific method Caffey started to take a critical view of the process of medical diagnosis and court response to injured children. In 1972, he wrote "On the Theory and Practice of Shaking Infants, Its Potential Residual Effects of Permanent Brain Damage and Mental Retardation." Doctor Caffey noted a growing awareness of the intentional inflictions of injuries to children. Referring to what he termed "parent-infant stress syndrome or battered bay syndrome."

Caffey moved from his first cautious tentative findings of potential abuse on the bodies of children to a more confident and mature advocacy for medical activism on behalf of children. He wrote in 1974 with this mature assurance in a work entitled "The Whiplash Shaken Infant Syndrome Manual Shaking by the Extremities with Induced Intracranial Bleedings, Linked with Residual Permanent Brain Damage and mental Retardation." Caffey wrote "Our evidence, both direct and circumstantial, indicates that whiplash shaking of infant s is a common primary type of trauma in the so-called battered infant syndrome. It appears to be the major cause in those infants who suffer from subdural hematomas and in intraocular bleedings." Caffey's writings have taken on a new direction, having in 1946 looking at long bone fractures he has moved in the 1970s to look at head injuries with greater potential for mental impairment and death. His writing also became more insistent in its power to teach and to warn those who would consider the findings on these children. The trajectory of Caffey's thinking becomes clear when one examines his further comments in that same year regarding his conclusion that this problem called for a nationwide movement to address this danger. He wrote "Current evidence, though manifestly incomplete and largely circumstantial, warrants a nation-wide educational campaign on the potential patho-genicity of habitual, manual, casual whiplash shaking of infants, and on all other habits, practices and procedures in which the heads of infants are habitually jerked and jolted (whiplash)."

This arc of Caffey's thinking from the first tentative questions about broken long bones, to concern for head injuries and finally to advocacy on behalf of children to prevent injuries and death through whiplash injuries elegantly captures the kind of development in knowledge that can occur in legal and scientific collaboration. Caffey's work never lost sight of the critical scientific analysis of x-ray data but it moved beyond single findings to concluding general trends in children's health care that needed to be addressed on a broad policy basis. This development keeps the best of critical scientific thinking and adds to it the experience of law and finally public policy. In this way Caffey's thinking reaches its logical conclusion from the specific, case by case finding of unexplained breaks in bones to the general, a broad social/public health problem of mishandling of children resulting in injury and death. In Caffey, we see the kind of leadership that scientists can bring to the service for children. Caffey's work continues to inform and motivate other who would testify in court to show abuse of children as my elderly pediatrician so eloquently did in educating me and through me in educating the court to the facts of abuse of our little boy, our victim/survivor

Finally Caffey's work in this x-ray evidence as it expressed itself through our pediatrician allowed me to present a case without the testimony of the child victim, who was in fact too young to be able to testify for himself. This is for me the most compelling reason to seek out expert testimony for children, it allows these cases of abuse to be prosecuted by other witnesses even when the victims are unable to testify for themselves. This is Caffey's greatest legacy his research and writing educated other scientists/doctors, in particular my doctor in my case. Through his work, Caffey encourages my doctor to give voice in court, detailing the broken bones of one little boy who could not speak for himself. Caffey and my doctor's voices were loud and clear, through their voices, their teaching, their advocacy our little boy's needs for protection was heard. This is an impressive legacy to give to American courts.

Chapter VIII
Biological and Chemical Abuse of Children

The ghost in William Shakespeare's Hamlet gives us a most chilling description of poisoning.

> Sleeping within my orchard, my custom always of the afternoon. Upon my secure hour thy uncle stole, with juice of cursed hebona in a vial, and in the porches of my ears did pour the leprous distilment, whose effect holds such an enmity with blood of man. That swift as quicksilver it courses through the natural gates and alleys of the body, and with a sudden vigor it doth (posset) and curd, like eager droppings into milk, the thin and wholesome blood. So did it mine, and a most instant tetter barked about, most lazar-like, with vile and loathsome curst all my smooth body.

Shakespeare has given us a description of a poisoning that is a road map for understanding the biological and chemical abuse of children. Three points in the ghost's account of his poisoning stand out in the most cruel poisoning of children. First like the ghost the poisoning of children often occurs in a time and place of apparent safety and assumed innocence. For the ghost he is in his beloved orchard "my orchard" and he is "sleeping." For children, their poisoning and abuse we will see most often occurs at home or even in a hospital where one would expect only safety and innocence.

Secondly, the ghost's poisoning like the poisoning of children occurs at the hand of a family member. For the ghost he is poisoned by his own brother's hand" for the children harmed in this way families, mother or father or another person charged with the child's care are most frequently found to be the ones responsible for this abuse. Finally the ghost's body is transformed "with vile and loathsome crust all my smooth body." For the child it is the same harm to that "smooth body" that the poison so powerfully affects. The smooth body of the ghost and that smooth body of the young child are both ravaged and ultimately destroyed.

In line with this pattern of poisoning of children Samuel X. Radbill wrote of the impact on the lives of children in the chapter "Children in a World of Violence: A History of Child Abuse in the 1987 book The Battered Child. Radbill's history noted the reports of the harm done to unborn children in the 1700s and 1800s in England. He wrote about the injury to these children through the mother's ingestion of alcohol while pregnant as well as the neglect by failed nurturing of children by these same alcohol consuming mothers. The scientific testimony of testing for blood alcohol content clearly would not have been available to courts in that early period but observations by third parties of alcohol consumption, intoxication and impairment in a mother's care for a child through intoxication could be presented to a court in those years as they could be today. This kind of evidence that raises the possibility of poisoning a child in utero becomes a crucially important matter in later years when chemical analysis of alcohol abuse becomes available. Like the ghost in Hamlet Radbill provides us with a similar pattern of abuse by poisoning of an innocent, at the hands of a family member, a mother and finally an injury to the body of the child through the poisoning, the corruption of that oh so "smooth body." It is important to note in this very early state of a historical response to poisoning of children that a frame work for protecting children from this harm has been established. The parent engages in dangerous behavior with a potentially toxic substance, that substance is brought to impact on the body of a child and a third party having knowledge of these things makes observation and shares these observations with a court. In this respect the observer offers what courts refer to as lay witness opinions which fall below the reach of an expert scientific opinion. Such opinions have been allowed to include an opinion from a person not qualified as an expert that another person is drunk. This is the kind of testimony, again it should be noted, that could come into court in the 1700s and the also today.

Radbill's work in this area carried on with his discussion of parental neglect while intoxicated in a practice known as overlaying. In overlaying, as it occurred in 1600s England small children were accidentally suffocated in bed by one of their parents who was intoxicated. Radbill wrote that this practice involved child victims many of whom were under a month old. The suffocation of these children occurred Radbill noted in the context of the parents intoxication. While the children in these situations were not poisoned, the precarious nature of children's lives in that time and the need for intervention and protection was evident. That children could die in this way and that children continued to die in this way well into the 1900s, as in 1920 the city of Birmingham, England reported no less than twenty such deaths, makes the need for court intervention by expert testimony all the more compelling. These historical reports express something more though beyond the pattern of neglect which I think goes directly to the heart of the need for scientific and legal collaboration and that is the extreme vulnerability of children. When we discuss the admission of scientific evidence and the great individuals who have advanced this scientific/legal effort as well as all the other important technical points that go along with this it is so important not to lose sight of the whole reason to improve this effort and that is for the well being of some very precariously placed children. I suspect that for each person, lawyer or scientist who became involved in this work there must have been a moment when he or she had to consider the injury and death of a young child. If people act out of their own self-interest I believe that they can also act out of an interest for the care of others. In the final analysis it is the ability to look beyond self-interest to the protection of others that distinguishes this work. The use of reason to care for those most vulnerable of persons makes this effort truly noble.

Closely allied to these cases of alcohol poisoning and over laying is the matter of harmful ingestions of other drugs by pregnant women. This matter of ingestion of drugs in particular illegal drugs by pregnant women moved front and center in public awareness in America in the past decades of the late 20th century. Consider the story of one person accused in the poisoning of a child and how the court responded. In the case of Daria D. v. Superior Court, from the state of California in 1998, we know that Daria and Vincent were addicted to heroin. To this couple was born a child named Casey, born prematurely on December 16, 1996 and at birth showing signs of drug withdrawal. At this point the chemists involved enter the story as Casey was tested and found to be positive for methadone, heroin and morphine. Casey's father Vincent admitted to his own history of drug use and to his failure to stop the child's mother Daria from using drugs during her pregnancy. The state of California filed an action on Casey's behalf alleging the drug abuse of Casey with the potential consequences of terminating the parental rights of Daria and Vincent. The state provided the parents with a reunification plan that concentrated on drug treatment and abstinence from drugs. In a six-month review hearing for this case the court ruled by a clear and convincing evidence standard, that the parents failed to participate in court ordered services. The court went on the find that the return of Casey to the parents would create a substantial risk to the child and finally that there was no substantial probability that Casey would be placed with the parents within the twelve months provided by law for the resolution of this kind of abuse case. The parents challenged the courts rulings saying that they deprived her of her substantive due process and also that the courts action deprived the mother the equal protection of the law. The court responded that in the cases of very young children like Casey it was permissible to move in this way and in this time frame to provide for a timely resolution of a permanent plan for Casey's future, would she be returned to her parents or would she be removed from her parents' custody and ultimately adopted. What I want to note in all of this is the importance of the chemical testing for drugs in Casey's body. The courts discussion of the cases stresses the parent's rights to constitutional protection and the speed at which courts need to move in these cases but none of this would have been possible without the scientific evidence from the chemical analysis of Casey's blood. It is so routine, indeed it is so accepted that in this case history, the drug evidence was not contested or even extensively commented on. This is important in that it suggest that courts, like this one have come to accept and in a routine way rely on such scientific evidence. The scientist, presumably a technician trained in chemistry and in drug testing, is not even named in the reporting of the case and it is likely that his or her test results were admitted into evidence without the technician even needing to be present, rather a certified report is often admitted without opposition. This reliance on the routine admission of scientific evidence tells us how important scientific evidence and the collaboration of lawyers and scientists has become in America. Quite simply put courts could not do their daily business without this kind of evidence. That admission of such evidence as routine, speaks volumes about how American Courts have embraced this process of scientific/legal collaboration and it suggests how much this process will expand in the years ahead as new findings in science make new evidence available to American courts.

In the final matter in this chapter regarding the poisoning of children and the scientific and legal response to those cases consider the case of People v. Phillips from the state of California in the year 1981. The Phillips case details a report of a strange phenomenon known as "Munchausen's Syndrome by Proxy" is presented. Just a few words at this point need to be said about this syndrome. Reported in a number of medical journals including the British medical journal Lancet. This is a rare and bizarre matter in which a caregiver for a child either poisons or causes other serious biological injuries to a young child under care. The unique twist to this is that the offending caretaker often reports the unexplained injuries to doctors and nurses while hiding the fact of their involvement in the abuse while gaining emotional comfort for being a kind and protective caregiver to the poisoned or injured child. This bizarre syndrome is as said before rare. In my career of twenty five years in which I handled several thousand child abuse matters I encountered only one case of this syndrome. The extreme rarity of this syndrome coupled with the medical and legal community's response is informative about how we handle all cases concerning child abuse. As a prosecutor I was called upon to lecture on child abuse cases to lawyers and the public in my county, my state and at national conferences. As a student of child abuse matters, I attended a number of state and national conferences in addition to lecturing in the 1980s and 1990s. In many of these conferences over those years, frequently one or more conference presenters was called upon to lecture about "Munchausen's Syndrome by Proxy" to the great interest and fascination of the conference attendees. In frequency these highly unusual cases frankly did not merit the time given to their presentation. A prosecutor could spend a whole career without encountering this syndrome even once and there were so many other cases that prosecutors needed to know about because they would see them like sexual abuse, broken bones and drug ingestion by pregnant mothers effecting children. The interest in this syndrome was perhaps that of a "side show" element of the odd and near unimaginable, but I believe that the interests in this matter came out of a common need of people to see and comprehend the unthinkable. These cases involved such deception on the part of parents linked to serious injury and even death of children that they are riveting to an observer but the added psychological need of the abuser for comfort and approval by unsuspecting medical staff makes this matter all the more repellant and at the same time intriguing. I believe at heart our fascination with this matter relates to a deeper need to understand how a human being can intentionally injury an innocent child. Note this syndrome usually occurs with very young, under one year old children. In these cases as we huddled around a lecturer who detailed the physical and psychological factors that led to people acting in such a strange ways, we were asking the same thing that we do of all expert scientific witnesses. "Explain to us what happened and explain to us why it happened" we asked. To anyone who has ever sat on a jury in a child abuse case in particular a child sexual abuse case by an adult there is at first on the jury's part great shock and amazement that such things can actually happen. In the experience of many Americans, these events of abuse have not occurred to them or their families and it is difficult for these jurors to imagine such unthinkable crimes. What the expert does here is explain the abuse and in so doing he or she makes that abuse comprehensible even if it is abhorrent. Expert witnesses can take us as they do into this syndrome into new realms of understanding by the very logic and reassurance of the language and logic of the scientific process. The scientist is a story teller and a comforter though not specifically intended because he or she "explains" the inexplicable.

Let us consider how this process of explanation occurs. In this case Priscilla Phillips, was described as a "kind, helpful and loving person, a dutiful wife to her husband, and a devoted mother of her two sons." Mrs. Phillips was reported to be an intelligent and educated woman with a Master's degree in social work. When she and her husband learned that they were unable to have children, they adopted a Korean born infant named Tia. The family and mother treated the child with care, getting her to pediatrician's appointments for care and treatment. Shortly after first taking Tia to the pediatrician Mrs. Phillips brought the infant back to the pediatrician and told the doctor that Tia had been violently vomiting and that she had a fewer. The cause of the vomiting and fever could not be determined at that time. Days later Tia was admitted to hospital for "starting spells." Doctors performed a wide range of chemical tests including blood sugar and blood calcium tests and a urine culture all of which failed to reveal any abnormalities. The hospital prepared to discharge Tia as her health had improve, but on the evening of her planned discharge she started to cry uncontrollably and could not be comforted. Tia started to vomit once again.

The child's diet was changed from regular baby formula to clear liquid, but she did not get better. The hospital then placed the child on intravenous fluids. The child improved and was again given clear liquids by mouth and the diarrhea started again. The feeding by mouth was again stopped and vomiting abruptly stopped and the child improved. This pattern continued and the doctors were unable to find a cause for these problems. The child's mother suggested to the doctors that her child, Tia, be placed on a regular diet which was done and she improved rapidly and was discharged.

A few days later the child was returned to the hospital with vomiting, diarrhea and extreme lethargy. Laboratory tests revealed that the little girl had extremely high levels of blood serum sodium and of bicarbonate. The doctors could not explain these findings. After her admission, Tia improved and she was again discharged. Finally, after a number of similar incidents of off again on again illness and cures in which chemical tests showed high blood levels of sodium and bicarbonate, Tia was admitted to the hospital one last time in critical condition and she died.

A few months after Tia's death the dead child's mother and her husband adopted another Korean infant named Mindy, and shortly after the same on again off again pattern of normal health followed by illness with excessive levels of blood sodium and hospitalization was observed in this second child. The doctors were stunned that the child could apparently have the same medical condition as Tia. They were not related in any way. Finally, the doctors came to the suspicion that the children had been poisoned. One of the doctors located an article in the British Medical Journal, Lancet, concerning this phenomena known as "Munchausen's Syndrome by Proxy." In that paper, a psychiatrist stated that the syndrome is one in which an individual either directly or through the vehicle of a child feigns, stimulates, or describes the dynamic similar to those in Tia's death. By proxy one simply means that instead of the person making themselves ill, they go through the psychodynamic process through the illness of another person as here in the illness of Tia and then the illness of Mindy. This action is often done by a child's mother who is outwardly devoted to the child and this happens when the child is very young, usually less than two years of age. Mental health experts have opined that the person who abuses a child in this fashion will typically transfer some unmet psychological needs onto pediatricians, nurses, and others through the care and approval they receive during "the illness" of this sick child.

The doctors discovered that the mother, who was later charged and convicted in the death of Tia and attack on Mindy, had won the support and trust of the medical staff for her care of children. Unbeknownst to the medical staff, the mother had been poisoning the children by putting massive amounts of sodium in the children's formula. These matters were brought to the attention of the local police and prosecuting attorneys and the woman was convicted of the murder of Tia and the attack on Mindy.

In examining this case one sees that a range of experts were needed to present this matter to the court. First the prosecutors used experts in chemical analysis to show that one child had sickened and died by extraordinarily high levels of sodium and that the other child also had these extraordinarily high levels of sodium. Coupled with this expert chemical analysis testimony was the evidence from the doctors and nurses who found the mother surreptitiously placing sodium into the second child's food. Finally the prosecutors introduced testimony from experts in mental health who were able to describe the psychological dynamic of Munchausen's Syndrome by Proxy to the jury.

This process of expert testimony along with non expert testimony of the defendant's action resulted in the woman's conviction. In this case, the expert can help a lawyer to bring to a conclusion a case that could not otherwise be prosecuted. This is the collaboration that I seek to encourage.

Chapter IX
Bite Mark Evidence

One early morning a few years ago in a clean, bright and well lit supermarket where my family and I shopped another family, a man and women with two little girls were wheeling their shopping carriage down the well stocked food isles picking up household items and filling their cart. At the store's meat counter the man and woman picked out expensive cuts of meat and later secreted them away in their clothes and then made their way with the little girls to the check out counter. The family moved through the check out counter paying only for the cheaper household items and not paying for the hidden meats. As they made their way out of the supermarket they were stopped by the store's security staff and detained. The local police were called and the man and woman were placed under arrest for shoplifting. The little girls, so young that they both were still in diapers were now separated from the man and woman, who were taken away in a police cruiser. Left with the two infant girls, the police, one might say, did what any good law enforcement officer would do in this case. In the language of too many police television shows to count, they "called for backup." They called for assistance from the police department's police matron, asking her to respond to the supermarket. The hapless officers, one can only imagine, were duely relieved on the arrival of the matron and on their opportunity to turn over their young charges, the two little girls, now with dirty diapers and all to the matron for her care. For the matron who had done these things all before this was routine. She came armed with the tools if not the weapons of her trade, diapers and baby wipes and set to the job at hand. All of this changed very quickly.

As the matron took the little girls' diapers off to clean them and to prepare them to be taken to the state's waiting social workers, she was stunned. Each little girls' genetalia were peppered with bright red angry marks that must have been sore and painful to look at for the matron and doubly sore and painful for the little girls to withstand. The matron gently cleaned the little girls, comforting them as best as she could, and she quickly drove them to the emergency room of the nearby university hospital. On arrival the little girls were met by nurses and doctors who were also stunned at first with the clearly painful injuries to the little girls. The hospital staff gathered its composure and quickly summonsed the hospital's photographer to photograph in color, with a good quality 35 mm camera each little girl's injuries. The photographer included a standardized color gauge which would later attest to the photographic accuracy of the angry red marks on each child's body and also included was a standard metric measuring gauge which would serve as a future guide to the size of the injuries. But what were those marks?

At the hospital the doctors had a suspicion that the marks on the little girls might be human bite marks, that's why they were so careful to document the marks photographically. Once the little girls were checked and treated they were placed in the care of the state's social service agency. The police, in conjunction with the District Attorney's Office, contacted the state's forensic dentist, an experienced expert witness in this field who had served in the military for a number of years during which he identified deceased military personnel who died in airplane crashes. I met with this forensic dentist and shared the police reports and hospital photographs to the little girls' injuries.

The woman who we learned was the mother of the little girls and her boyfriend were held on bail for the shoplifting charge with an additional charge of assault and battery filed against both mother and her boyfriend. At this stage we needed to provide our dentist with further evidence and to do this I filed a court document seeking to have the two defendants bite mark impressions taken. The Untied States Constitution prohibits the compulsory taking of testimonial evidence from a defendant, but it does allow the taking of non-testimonial evidence from a defendant such as blood samples, saliva and as in this case the taking of dental impressions of each defendant's mouth. At this stage the defendants, the mother, and her boyfriend were represented by lawyers and their lawyers did not object to the taking of the bite mark impressions understanding that the court would order the defendants to submit to the procedure even if they objected. Our forensic dentist prepared a substance that was placed into the defendant's mouths, which hardened and yielded an exact mold of their mouths, in particular their teeth. Using a reverse mold the dentist then made an exact model of the defendant's teeth. Using the model of the defendant's teeth the dentist matched them to the photographs of the bite marks of the children's genetalia. The dentist reached the opinion that the bite marks on each child had been made exclusively by the mother's boyfriend.

The dentist's opinion then became the basis of my case. Because teeth, life fingerprints, are unique to each person, our dentist was able to say with reasonable scientific certainty that the boyfriend had inflicted the bite marks. The boyfriend pled guilty and received a jail sentence while the mother pled guilty to a statute that was in effect at that time for failure to protect her children from harm and was placed on probation. The state's social service agency continued to provide care for the little girls.

Just as this story changed with the discovery of the bite marks on the little girls so too did the direction and outcome of this case change because we had an expert witness. Without this expert we would have been unable to prosecute these defendants. The little girls were too young to be able to testify to the injuries and to the identity of their attacker. This story of our two little girls led me to write this book. I was so impressed that I was able to prosecute this case though expert evidence in spite of the unavailability of the children that I started to look for other cases in which we could use scientific evidence to protect children when those children could not go to court and testify to protect themselves. I knew that there would be a limited number of cases like this where we could conduct a successful prosecution without a child witness but I was excited about the possibility of stretch the bounds and number of these cases. Shortly after this case I looked for a way to encourage this kind of legal and scientific collaboration, and to achieve that goal I started work on this book with the students and staff of Worcester Polytechnic Institute where I had previously worked as a professor.

In considering this story of bite mark evidence, I am first and foremost struck with the network of protection available for these children. From the store security staff person to the police officer to the police matron, there were people who watch over the children and gave them the best care that they could. That network of care extended into the University hospital where the nurses and doctors recognized the trauma to the little girls and treated them. Added to this case the hospital photographer extended that care and in so doing set the stage for a forensic response to the injuries of these little girls. The missing link could have been the identification of the bite marks but that was also in place. The dental expert could distinguish between animal and human bite marks and finally moved the case forward by saying that the bite marks actually came from the defendant. The presence of this expert meant that this network of protective care was available. The last steps with this evidence were in hindsight the easiest of steps. When confronted with the order to give up his bite mark pattern he did not resist and when confronted with the evidence that he was the biter, again he chose not to resist and plead guilty. In this book I have, from time to time, talked about the chaos and unsettling condition of child abuse from serious injury and in some cases death. What this network of care does is to push back that chaos and make order out of the chaos. From the unthinkable, of a grown man actually biting the bodies of little children who could not resist, some measure of order is returned as a rational reasoning person, the expert explains what has happened and in so doing returns some measure of order and safety for the children. This return to order and balance is a recurrent theme for me as we talk about this scientific evidence. If the criminal act is the triumph of the disordered and chaotic the rational testimony of the scientists is the triumph of reason. This network of care worked because of the scientists involved.

The fact that no child needed to testify in this case is the next extraordinary point that I wish to note. For a prosecutor, for this prosecutor the most difficult task is the presentation of a child witness to a court. The reasons are these. First, some children like these little girls are just too young to be able to testify against their abusers. Secondly, children even when able to testify are not automatically assumed to be competent to testify and must be found to be competent to testify based on a showing of an understanding on the child's part of their responsibility to tell the difference between the truth and an awareness of the consequences for not telling the truth. Finally for children, testifying in court is just so hard to do. The court room is not set up to put child witnesses at ease, the person accused of abusing a child is going to be in the same room as the child reporting the abuse and the child is questioned by an adult, a lawyer about personal and sensitive matters. To be able to put a child abuse case to trial without needing the child witness is just about the best thing that can happen to me as a prosecutor. In these cases you have prosecuted the defendant and you have not had to potentially traumatize a child by having him or her testifying.

This story of our little girls and our forensic dentist makes me look for other cases where we can put our cases forward without the need for a child witness. These cases are unfortunately all too rare. For example in a child rape case the prosecutor usually has the word of the child victim against the word of the defendant. It then became my goal in writing this book to put this story and the story of other men and women-scientific experts who came teach other scientists how to do this work. It was my hope and it remains my hope that someone reading this story working perhaps in a research lab will be struck by the possible application of his or her work like our dentist to serve children in an American court through his or her expertise.

In closing, I would note the importance in this story of one person providing care to another. The scientist in this case never met the little girls or knew them in any way, yet with the application of his knowledge and skill, he cared for them like all of those others in that network. He, through his actions, made their lives safer and better. From a story that started in pain and chaos, the story ends not in perfection or perfect order but it ends in at least a chance for safety and care for these children because of this scientist.

Chapter X
Cameras and Technology in Courts

When asked by a reporter about the possibility that the new Chief Justice of the United States Supreme Court might some day allow Supreme Court cases to be televised Supreme Court Justice Antonin Scalia responded, "Not a chance, because we don't want to become entertainment. I think there's something sick about making entertainment out of real people's legal problems. I don't like it in the lower court, and I don't particularly like it in the Supreme Court."

Justice Scalia may not have been speaking for the Chief Justice here, indeed time will answer, that but he does represent his own views and the views of many in the judiciary in their response to public access to American courtrooms. Public access be it by television or other means has always been a concern of courts as they seek to balance the real need to insulate the decision-making process of courts from undue public pressure against the public's right to know and be informed about important government matters including court decisions. Perhaps Justice Scalia's comments missed the point of the public's need to know how the court operates by confusing that with entertainment. From a practicing lawyer's point of view and law professor's point of view, both mine, I have found lawyers, law students and members of the public to be absolutely reverent and spell-bound to the playing, which I have done for members of each of these groups of tapes of the oral arguments of important Supreme Court cases. Easily among my best attended and best received law school classes is the one in which I play the tape recording of the oral argument in the case of Roe v. Wade. Students who think they know the case, who have read the decision, discussed it, analyzed the opinion, and convinced themselves that they "know the case" are completely undone by hearing the actual words of the lawyers and the judges echoing off the walls of the Supreme Court room. Most people don't realize that the court ordered a rare second round of oral arguments in part because the court knew how important the decision would be and the tapes reveal that. Law students are stuck because the decision never told them that when the lawyer for Roe, Sarah Weddington, sat down after arguing the first time, the lawyer for the state made what could be seen as a patronizing and sexist comment to his opposing counsel which was met with stone silence from the Supreme Court bench. My point is that the new technology here, the new media in this case the tape recording of the court proceeding provided subtle insight into the case that would have been missed by having access to only a written record. With all due respect to Justice Scalia this is not entertainment for these American law students rather it is critical information for them in understanding this case and reaching their own informed judgment, what ever that judgment may be about Roe v. Wade.

The concept I wish to explore here is the balance of court's need for maintaining the proper distance from public exposure against the public's legitimate need to know about the operations of government. This balance can I believe be best explored by an examination of the pluses and minuses to be seen in the handling of video taping and other forms of new technology as used in the area of child abuse cases in American courts. Justice Scalia's words should make us think carefully about how best to balance these interests. In this area we need to be concerned with Justice Scalia's insistence with tradition but that awareness cannot stifle informed and thoughtful innovation. Just like playing a tape recording of an oral argument for law students is an innovation. That innovation can give depth and understanding to the older technology of the printed word. Courts have considered new and innovative ways of taking testimony from children in sensitive child abuse and this new innovation like the tape recording needs to play its role in service to children in American courts.

In the United States Supreme Court case of Coy v. Iowa decided in 1988 we see a state and the Supreme Court struggling with what is the proper balance between tradition and innovation. In this case the state of Iowa passed a law that allowed courts to place a special screen between the child witness in child abuse cases and the adult defendants who were on trial. In the case the defendant was accused of sexually assaulting two thirteen-year-old girls. The Iowa law allowed the children known as the complaining witnesses to testify either by a closed-circuit television system or from behind this screen that provided for one way viewing, that is the children could not see the defendant but the defendant, his lawyer and the jury could see the children. This screen for our purposes can be seen as a "new technology," An innovation seeking to ease the anxiety of the child witnesses in testifying against the adult defendant. This was an innovation like the innovation of the tapes of the oral arguments was in the education of young lawyers. The tradition and the traditional way that this evidence was presented in American courts is by face to face testimony of the child given in the presence of the defendant. So important was this tradition of "face to face" confrontation, the Supreme Court had ruled that the defendant's Sixth Amendment rights mandated to "face to face" process for the taking of evidence in a criminal trial. The Sixth Amendment, part of the first ten amendments to the Constitution (the Bill of Rights) which was ratified effective on December 15, 1791 provides in pertinent part "In all criminal prosecution, the accused shall enjoy...to be confronted with the witness against him... ." This language was later found to require the actual "face to face" confrontation of accused and defendant.

The facts in this case are these. The defendant was arrested and charged with sexually assaulting two thirteen-year old girls. They reported that the defendant sexually assaulted them while they were camping out in a tent in their own backyard. The defendant's home was adjacent to the girl's home. The girls told the police and so testified at trial that their attacker entered their tent after they had gone to sleep for the night. The girls were greatly fearful of the defendant at the time of the attack and at the time of trial. The girls reported that their attacker entered their tent wearing a stocking over his head to obscure his identity. The girls went on to say that their attacker shined a flashlight in their eyes and warned them not to look at him. The girls were unable to describe their attacker's face. At the start of the trial the prosecution moved to have the court allow the girls to testify either by closed-circuit television or from behind the special one-way screen. The special one-way screen was eventually used. The defendant was convicted on these charges.

On appeal the defendant argued that the use of the screen between the young girls and himself denied him his constitutionally protected right to "face to face" confrontation with his accusers. The defendant also argued that the special screen required changes in the courtroom lighting to operate (the lights had to be turned way down and the windows were draped). The defendant argued that these charges caused him to be inherently prejudiced by this procedure in front of the jury and that this caused a perception of his guilt that improperly worked against him in his trial. The Supreme Court on appeal of the defendant's conviction ruled in favor of the defendant. The court's opinion stated "The remaining questions is whether the right to confrontation was in fact violated in this case... It is difficult to imagine a more obvious or damaging violation of the defendant's rights to a face-to-face encounter." The Court noted that because there was not an individualized finding that the girls were not able to testify in the defendant's presence without being harmed, a process that the court in Iowa failed to do the defendant's conviction could not be upheld.

In a concurring opinion (a separate decision from the courts majority decision that agrees with the majority but reaches that position through another path of legal reasoning), Justice Sandra Day O'Connor wrote an important opinion that sought to support the Court's decision striking down the defendant's conviction, while still keeping open the option of future innovation by new technology in the admission of child abuse case evidence. Justice O'Connor wrote "I agree with the court that appellant's rights under the confrontation clause were violated in this case." Justice O'Connor then explained her view that the attempt to find innovative ways of introducing might some day be found and perhaps that innovation would not offend against the Constitution as the special screen had. Justice O'Connor wrote "I write legally only to vote my view that these rights are not absolute but rather may give way in an appropriate case to other competing interests so as to permit the use of certain procedural devices designed to shield a child witness from the trauma of courtroom testimony." Note that lawyers usually refer to "procedural devices" as a legal construct or argument that advances a litigant's theory of the law to his or her advantage. I suggest that Justice O'Connor saw this term "procedural device" in a much more expansive way, a way we will see that included new technologies for the acceptance of evidence into courts.

In just two short years after the Coy decision, the Supreme Court was to return to this question of "face to face" confrontation and innovation in "procedural devices" by the case of Maryland v. Craig in the year 1990.

In the Craig case, Shandra Ann Craig was charged with various sex offenses against a six-year-old girl who attended a kindergarten program owned and operated by the defendant. When the case went to trial, the prosecution elected to use a Maryland statute that allowed a judge to receive a child witness testimony by way of a one-way closed circuit television. To use this new technology, the trial judge had to make a specific finding that this child would suffer serious emotional distress so that the child could not reasonably communicate. The practical result of the court's decision was that the prosecutor and defense attorney went to a room separate from the courtroom to question the child. The judge, jury and defendant stayed in the courtroom and the questioning of the little girl was televised into the courtroom. The defense attorney had a microphone that allowed communication between the defendant and defense counsel during the child's questioning. The child witness could not see the defendant.

Expert testimony was offered from a psychologist for the state to show that if forced to testify in front of the defendant, the little girl would experience great harm. Based on this expert testimony, the judge was able to conclude that the particularized finding of harm to the child witness if she testified fact-to-face with the defendant in the state statute was met. It should be remembered that in the earlier case of Coy v. Iowa a televised system was available to the state but the state used its special one way viewing screen. The screen it should be recalled was held by the Supreme Court to violate the requirement of face-to-face confrontation found in the Sixth Amendment of the Constitution.

Here one sees that kind of shift in a court's thinking that so holds our collective public attention. Rather than striking down the use of the closed circuit television finding that it operated like the screen in violating the face-to-face aspect of the confrontation clause the Supreme Court upheld the State's use of the technology of the close circuit television. Crucial to remember her is that the judge unlike the judge in Coy made a particularized finding based on expert testimony that the child would be harmed without special arrangement being made to take her testimony. Writing for the majority Justice O'Connor wrote that "...a defendant's right to confront accusatory witnesses may be satisfied absent a physical, face-to-face confrontation at trial only where denial of such confrontation is necessary to further an important public policy and only where the reliability of the testimony is otherwise assured."

Justice O'Connor had written in the Coy case that she ruled against the state's use of the one way screen, but she did so mindful that she wished not to stop states from experimenting with new ways of helping child witnesses in abuse cases to be able to give their testimony. I am struck by the leadership of Justice O'Connor in these two decisions as she works her way through what many in the defense and the prosecution bars felt would be a clear rejection of closed circuit television based on the face-to-face requirement for criminal presentations. Remember that in Coy while the children were behind a screen they were still in the same courtroom as the defendant and here in the Craig case the child was at all times out and away from the defendant, in a completely different room. Perhaps a key to understanding this decision lies in the person of Justice O'Connor and her ability to lead the court on children's issues. She had concerns about the screen procedure in Coy but she wrote in her concurring decision a message of encouragement for those who would seek to bring proper innovation into the court process...further Justice O'Connor's decision in Craig recognized the particularized finding of risk of harm to the little girl and her decision looks to see that "...the reliability of testimony is otherwise assured." In this sense Justice O'Connor may have addressed the proper use of cross-examination and other defense practices to assure a proper defense. Finally it is clear that Justice O'Connor in writing in both cases played a major role in shaping and forming the courts thinking of this issue of what can be characterized as a cautious innovation.

The balance of traditional practice and innovation is explored in these cases and by these judges. Running through these cases are the common threads of expert testimony and new technologies for presenting crucial evidence. The process of change is slow to some but I would suggest that it is certain. Recognizing the need to assist children, to give their testimony in these cases with the need to assure a constitutionally proper trial Justice O'Connor worked her way through the facts and law of each case that balanced both tradition and innovation. Television, a source of entertainment in the right hands, became a source of insight in the hands of another.

Chapter XI
Biochemical Evidence
of the Sexual Abuse of Children

Everyone enjoys a good mystery. Perhaps it's the thrill of the unknown, maybe it's the skill of the detective, but for me it always was the search for the elusive, if not metaphorical, "fingerprint" that when discovered, solves the mystery. In this vein I suggest the body of new research that has disclosed that young girls who have been sexually abused have significantly altered body chemistry very much like the body chemistry of soldiers who have gone through a harrowing combat experience and are suffering from posttraumatic stress. For me, this research is an extraordinary example of the hidden, or, as fingerprint examiners names it, "the latent prints" at a crime scene. If found this evidence, which will be discussed here in some depth, is mysterious because it has apparently always been there in the bodies of sexual abuse victim, unknown and just waiting for us to discover. The mystery and the significance of this new research is also to be found in the fact that while these body changes have been found to occur, scientists have not aggressively pushed prosecutors to exploit them as a new and promising tool in prosecuting child abuse cases. This lack of linkage, if you will between a new scientific discovery and a quick comprehension to that discoveries application to help in children's cases in court was in itself a major reason for the writing of this book. The application of this connection leaps out to me as a way of supporting a child witnesses' testimony of having been sexually abused. Assume that you have a child who is able to say that she has been sexually abused, the finding that her body chemistry is like that of a soldier experiencing post traumatic stress, could give a prosecutor physical evidence to support the child's claim. Following this image of a mystery the abnormalities in the body chemistry of these children could be the detective's last clue in closing out a case. The fact that this scientific finding has been in existence all along is for me personally very powerful and prophetic. For many years after prosecuting child abuse cases in which all I had was the word of the child victim against that of the adult defendant's aggressive denial and then having lost my case, I was left alone, wondering, wasn't there some missing evidence, some mystery "fingerprint," some "latent print" that would reveal the abuse that we had all just missed. I remember this sense of deep frustration would follow me for days after I had lost one of these cases. With this new set of research findings, it may now be possible to solve at least some of these mysteries, these unresolved cases.

The journal of the American Academy of Adolescent Psychiatry published an article in 1994 that clarified this discussion for me of solving child abuse cases through the "latent fingerprint" of biochemical changes in children's bodies. The article "Urinary Catecholamine Excretion in Sexually Abused Girls" raised for me the hope of finding this "latent fingerprint."

The researchers in this study started with a definition of childhood sexual abuse as severe and/or repeated adverse sexual abuse experience(s) involving genital contact by an older perpetrator against a child under age eighteen. They further noted that such abuse was frequently marked by increased psychiatric morbidity including depression, dysthmia, suicidal ideation and suicide attempts. Finally, the authors took special note of the fact that extensive psychological and psychiatric studies had been done concerning childhood sexual abuse and that little is known about the biological impact of such sexual abuse.

What was known about the biological effects of sexual abuse included the fact that stress like that which would occur in child sexual abuse will produce increased levels of norepinephrine. Other changes noted in clinical studies included findings that uncontrollable stress results in increased responsiveness of locus ceruleus neurons, the primary location of norepinephrine activity in the brain.

With this information the researchers developed a method for their study. The scientists studied forty-two girls (20 abused 22 control). The girls were recruited for the study of urinary concentrations of selected chemicals that are associated with elevated levels of stress (catecholamine). The sexually abused girls were recruited from Child Protective Services of the Washington, D. C. area. The non-abused control subjects were recruited through advertisements and they were matched with the abused subjects as to age, socioeconomic status, race, and family structure (one or two parent families). Thirty-one girls (16 abused, 15control) participated in initial urinary screening. The method called upon all the subjects to submit to routine blood drawings, to give a detailed medical history and to take a physical examination performed by a female examiner. As the study continued, three of the subjects did not continue with the testing (2 abused, 1 control). Researchers also ranked the girls on the Tanner scale based on breast and pubic hair development. Other data including psychiatric data when available and testing for childhood depression was also done. The results of the initial screening was that the abused group of girls showed no significant difference from the control group of girls in age, race, Tanner (sexual development) stage, height, body weight, body surface area, family structure and childhood depression scores. Further, all the young girls were found to be living in stable homes for one year before the start of the testing. As to difference, a greater rate of suicide ideation, suicide attempts and dysthymia was noted in the sexually abuse girls than in the control girls.

Turning to the reports of the sexually abused girls, the study found that the mean age for the girls of the start of their sexual abuse was 6.3 years ± 2.4years. The duration of the sexual abuse was 22.1 months 2 months with a mean time since disclosure of the abuse of 5.2 years to 3.5 years. All of the cases of sexual abuse involved physical contact of the girls' genitals with 42% of the girls presenting vaginal and/or anal penetration. All of the girls' abusers were male and known to the abused girls. Of the abusers 33% were fathers of the girls, 8% were stepfathers or mother's live-in boyfriend, and 58% were other known males including uncles, cousins and neighbors.

The researchers, in an attempt to further avoid error in their results excluded any significant medical" disorders, the talking of any meditation within three weeks of the catecholamine testing, obesity, IQ's below 70, positive urine pregnancy tests or suspected pregnancies, substance abuse, positive urine toxicology screens, and other medical treatments that might affect the girls' urine chemistry. With these precautions, the researchers had excluded as many variables as they could see and they were then ready to turn to the sampling and biochemical testing that would form the basis of their comparative testing of the two groups of abused and control girls. The researchers employed a uniform system for collecting urine samples. The girls and their guardians (parents, etc.) received specific instructions about the collection of 24-;-hour urine samples. The plan called for three to five consecutive 24-hour urine collections. The urine was to be refrigerated during the length of the collecting period. At the finish of the24-hour collection period the urine was evaluated for creatinine, a critical chemical in the study. The girls kept to their regular diet and physical activities. Finally, the mean of urinary catecholamine and melabolite concentrates were noted for each young girl. Gas chromatography was employed in the testing of the materials and specific levels of various catecholamines were calculated down to the micromole levels.

For statistical purposes the researchers calculated the mean ± standard deviations for concentrations of catecholamines and metabolites excreted .into urine per 24 hours.

The results of the chemical testing were that the sexually abused girls exhibited greater total catecholamine synthesis referred to as (Total CA) when compared with demographically matched control subjects- the non-sexually abused girls. The abused girls also urinated significantly higher levels of certain metabolite substances. These differences could not be explained by any variable such as height or age of the girls. The researchers noted that the sexually abused girls demonstrated greater total catecholamine synthesis (Total CA) as measured by various catecholamines and their metabolites when compared against demographically paired and matching control subjects, i.e., read in this context non-sexually abused girls. These findings could be seen as consistent with clinical findings on catecholamine levels in adult patients with post-traumatic stress disorder and also with adults and children experiencing major depression. The researchers noted that severe sexual abuse like that experienced by the sexually abused girls in the test is a disruptive experience that can lead to post-traumatic stress disorder. The researchers noted that the levels of these chemicals in the girls' urine resembled those levels found in psychobiological testing of post-traumatic stress disorder victims. Of special note in the study was the documented reports of elevated levels of urine with similar findings of these chemicals from Vietnam War combat veterans who demonstrated post-traumatic stress disorders. Clinical literature demonstrated raised sympathetic nervous system arousal in those soldiers suffering from post-traumatic stress disorders. The researchers noted that clinical studies indicated that uncontrollable stress results in increased responsiveness of certain points in the brain that are sensitive to excitory stimulation. From these similarities noted in the biochemical material in the urine of the sexually abused girls and the post-traumatic stress affected war veterans, the researchers concluded that sexually abused girls show higher catecholamine activity that was in some ways similar or one might say consistent with the psychobiology of both adult and childhood depression sufferers. The researchers noted that severe stress such as sexual assault in the early years of child hood as these girls reported could lead to alterations of catecholamine activity. The study also cautioned that one should not miss the significance of person's genetic make-up which might predispose a person to depression, suicidal thinking and other abnormalities of the nervous system.

The report concluded by stating that girls with histories of severe sexual abuse demonstrated increases in catecholamine production. The writers of, the study noted that to their knowledge such variations in these urine excretions had never been reported before. Further, the findings are consistent with the results of urine tests of adults reported in studies concerning post-traumatic stress disorders. The researchers conceded that they could not determine cause regarding the psychiatric symptoms and biochemical changes observed. The writers stated that their results needed to be interpreted with caution because of the admittedly small numbers of subjects in the control and test groups. Still the researchers pointed out that their results are in agreement with psychobiological models of post-traumatic stress disorders supported in preclinical and clinical literature. The researchers concluded that these sexually abused girls seem to demonstrate the same biological changes found in adults suffering from post-traumatic stress disorder without a finding of the full blown syndrome. The writers noted that their findings could also be seen as consistent with non-specific severe stressors other than sexual abuse. The researchers called for further investigation of the connection of severe stress such as child abuse on human development. The researchers recommended prospective longitudinal follow-up studies to be done. These studies would focus on the psychobiology and the psychopathology of children who have suffered from severe stress.

Researchers published their work in a journal discussing the findings of chemical differences between abused and non-abused girls. What is the significance of these successive studies in a phrase is peer review. It should be recalled that review - the publication of scientific research critical review by others in one's field is a hallmark of the scientific endeavor and that peer review critical to developing reliability in a scientific finding. We see, therefore, that the first and now second publication are part of that gradual process which important if this or other scientific finding sever be accepted in court for children's cases. By gaining approval of one's peers for their find these researchers can put themselves in a position to be able to fender their findings on abuse case

The importance of this should not be missed. The researchers themselves said that there is need for further study of this issue of chemical differences in the bodies of abused victims and non-abuse. The researchers cited the limited number of people in the sample as one area of concern and there would undoubtedly be outers. This willingness to submit one's ideas to criticism is vital to the whole of the collaborative process and it should be noted.

Finally, we will see that the researchers in this second article also failed to note the significance of their work to children in child abuse cases. This is the goal of this text—to get scientific researchers to reflect about their findings as they relate to the needs of children. If ever there was a question of the need to encourage this reflection in this way, these chemical findings and the absence of the researchers understanding of the potential value of their work in child abuse cases cries out for this kind of encouragement. Researchers also published their work in another study published in the Journal of Clinical Endocrinology and Metabolism. This second study of these matters (2) also explored the findings suggesting differences between the sexually abused and non-sexually abused girls. This study examined the operation of the hypothalamic-pituitary adrenal axis in thirteen sexually abused girls and thirteen control girls age 7 to age 15. This study used a technique that examined the response of blood cortisol and renocorticotrophic hormone (ACTH). The study worked on this axis which was a stress sensitive system that helps a person's body for the fight or flight response so very critical to human survival. In the comparison of controls to the abused girls the researchers found signs of disregulation of that axis and varied attempts in the children's bodies to compensate by keeping cortisol levels down. The study suggested that the children's bodies were trying to deal with added stress.

The researchers in this study bluntly stated that sexual abuse is not just a traumatic experience that results in psychiatric disorders but also it is an insult to the body which produces biological changes. The study went on to say that the age of the individual, the severity of the abuse, and the genetic make-up for the abused survivor may affect the extent of axis disregulation. Like the earlier study, this study noted that it could not determine the cause of the psychiatric and biological changes, noting that the abused girls who were in health care might have suffered prior maltreatment. They concluded their observations by noting that these biological findings may be of value to other professionals in understanding and treating depression in maltreated children.

These findings were consistent in both studies and supported one another.

What are we to make of these findings? First it must be noted that at no point did any of the researchers point to their work as biological proof that the girls in questions were sexually abused and of course we need not be surprised by that because their work was not to prove or to disprove that the girls were sexually abused. That point was in fact a given in their research.

Still the significance of such a finding and its potential for application for court cases was completely missed. This is exactly the point I am trying to make. This is the central point to the whole of this work, that next step application of new scientific finding should be being made. We are still working with professions who are thinking and responding only within their own professional horizon and such an obvious potential for a connection should be made. Scientists don't need to know the intricacies of legal proof, but in service to their profession, let alone to the people their research can serve, (children, in this case) they should be alert to these connections.

Further, let us examine this potential evidence in the scope of the new test for scientific evidence found in Daubert. If Daubert calls for relevancy and reliability, are we not already on the threshold of admitting such "evidence."?

First, as to relevance, has not the case been clearly made for that? Don't these biochemical findings have a direct bearing, a relevance to the question—has this child not been sexually abused? Are we not faced with telltale signs of abuse that are almost equivalent of fingerprints in a classic criminal case? If relevance is the first key to admission, would it not be possible for a scientist to describe these findings as they might appear in an individual child's tested urine, and say that such findings are consistent with abuse? Remember, the scientist would not, as both articles say, be able to address causation, that is, this person caused this abuse that caused this biochemical change. Rather, the scientists might say this child has biochemical findings that are consistent with being sexually abused. This, I suggest, is relevant. The child would still need to identify an abuser but the scientific testimony could support her evidence of in fact being abused.

If a requirement of scientific reliability is called for after relevancy, could this test also be met? The judge could hear testimony of these studies and related studies that had over and over linked changes as found in these tests to traumatic experiences. Could a judge find that scientists had concluded that such changes occur as a by-product or aftermath of sexual abuse and so find that such evidence could be admissible?

This then is the challenge of taking new scientific evidence and applying it to court cases. Is this material ready for presentation to a court today? The answer to that, I suggest under the current Daubert test, a relaxed and lower standard is yes. The debate still comes back to that essential need for scientists to be attuned to the potential applications of their work. The fields of research here are specialized that it is unlikely that the average trial attorney is going to come across such results. Conversely, there is an obligation for lawyers to keep alert to new developments that may be of help to their clients. Indeed, one line of reasoning could be that lawyers have an obligation to keep up-to-date in the law. Could it also be argued that lawyers would have an obligation to keep up-to-date in new scientific developments that might be of help for their clients? I do not want to push this point too far, Lawyers are not trained scientists, but an awareness of these fields to a general level may be part of the future for effective advocacy.

The potential is here for use of this new biochemical evidence in prosecution when found and in defense when not found in testing of children. Before the potential of court use comes into play, the need for true cross-disciplinary thinking about the application of these new findings must occur. That is indeed the future.

For me this "mystery" process is a deeply personal process for the protection of children. It is my deepest hope that this technology and other new technologies come to be part of that protective process for children.

Chapter XII
Conclusions

In this book I have attempted to tell a story based on my twenty-five years as a prosecutor, about a number of extraordinary people, trained in the sciences whose work has benefited countless numbers of children in American courts. I have intentionally tried to tell that story with an eye toward including my own personal involvement in some of those child abuse cases. I did this because I believed this would give some depth to these stories beyond a mere restatement of the law and science involved. Above all else I included my personal responses to the cases, such as a frustration after loosing a rape case, a sense of deep appreciation for a blunt but perceptive pediatrician/witness or a deep respect of the work of Doctor John Caffey because I believed these things might encourage others to act on behalf of children. This belief was at the very heart of this book's inception, a belief that people trained in the sciences have much to offer in understanding and even solving cases of child abuse. It is my belief that these people who I have written about can lead others to improve the protection of children through their work. In the next to the last chapter, Chapter XI, I have tried to write about an area of scientific research that has yet to be tapped for use in court. I am referring to the finding of chemical changes in the bodies of sexually abused children. The fact that there is a clear application of such evidence, to me a prosecutor, leads me to wonder why the scientists didn't see this potential application immediately. I hope to make such a process of application of technology to children's need a more common process. For persons trained in the sciences serving as an expert in the setting of a trial can be nerve racking and exhilarating and it was my hope that these stories would encourage scientifically trained person to pick up this challenge as so many other skilled practitioners have done. The chance to challenge one's knowledge in the context of a contested adversarial setting might not be for everyone but for those who would accept it, coupled with a belief that one's testimony could benefit others is exhilarating.

In this book I also set out to explore the similarities rather than the differences that scientists and lawyers share. In a time when public debate in so many areas of public matters seems to turn on conflict, it seemed wise if not slightly old-fashioned to suggest that we share with one another more that unites us than divides us. In this regard I am struck most by the historian of science Thomas Kuhn who understood the significance of "precedence" in both legal work and scientific work. Kuhn thought that precedence can be so important in advancing the day to day work or both the law and science but he also understood that both fields share the experience of new "paradigms," that is new scientific discoveries for the scientist or new law or court decision for the lawyer that shake and remake the way these professionals understand the world. I hoped, in this discussion of the shared intellectual heritage that both areas enjoy, to encourage others to see the joy in the work that comes from new knowledge and intellectual insight. This sense of joy is a gift for those who will look for it that comes out of the exercise of logic and reason that is directed by imagination and exploration. Just think for a moment that we might be able someday to find a tell tail touchstone to prove physical abuse in the bones or flesh of the very chemical make up of a child. The discovery and intelligent use of that knowledge is breath taking and it had kept me active and involved in this field of law for over twenty-five years. I hope that some of that personal and intellectual joy could be seen in these pages.

Finally this book looked to encourage others, doctors, engineers, chemists, lawyers, police officers, judges, therapists, and so many others to see their special unity and common purpose in serving others. This common purpose to serve is in my experience something that lawyers are frightened and shocked about openly discussing. Law sadly still remains in many ways a limited profession where one would never openly express one's feelings let alone one's feeling as a caregiver or protector. This is slowly changing yet still such a confession about one's desire to care is often seen as "weak" and "less than professional." But at the core of a lawyers work and at the core of a scientist's work lies a desire to learn and affect one's world. That focus on learning and effecting easily moves into commitment of service and care. My purpose here is to state and encourage that care. Consider in this regard Dr. Caffey's work as he went over archival x-rays of children's bodies. He did not set out to serve rather I suspect that he was more motivated by curiosity, but that curiosity lead him to insight (insight that children were being hurt and killed) and finally it lead him to advocacy and action. This is the kind of care for children that this book is meant to foster, a quiet intellectually driven move to help others. This drive is the best that law and science share and this drive is what these pages are meant to encourage.

Michael Edmond Donnelly
Paxton, Massachusetts 2006

WPI*Studies*

WPI Studies is sponsored by Worcester Polytechnic Institute, the nation's third oldest independent technological university. WPI Studies aims to publish monographs, edited collections of essays, and research tools and texts of interest to scholarly audiences. WPI Studies accepts manuscripts in all languages, and is especially interested in reviewing potential publications on interdisciplinary topics relating science, technology, and culture. WPI Studies is edited by a board of WPI faculty from many disciplines. The board is chaired by Lance Schachterle, Assistant Provost and Professor of English, to whom potential authors should direct their inquiries (WPI, Worcester, MA 01609).

To order other books in this series, please contact our Customer Service Department at:

800-770-LANG (within the U.S.)
212-647-7706 (outside the U.S.)
212-647-7707 FAX

or browse online by series at:

www.peterlang.com